Compilers
A High-Level Overview

By: J.J. F. Reibel

Contents

Chapter 5: Intermediate Code Generation

Chapter 6: Code Optimization

Chapter 7: Code Generation

Chapter 8: Run-Time Systems

Chapter 1: Introduction to Compilers

I. Introduction to compilers and their role in software development

In the ever-evolving landscape of software development, compilers stand as the unsung heroes, the hidden architects behind the scenes, shaping the way our digital world functions. They are the magicians that translate human-readable source code into the intricate dance of ones and zeros that our computers can comprehend. In this inaugural chapter, we embark on a journey into the fascinating realm of compilers, unearthing their profound significance in the world of software engineering.

The Genesis of Compilers:
Before we dive headfirst into the intricacies of compilers, let us first ponder the origins of these enigmatic entities. In the early days of computing, programmers had to communicate with machines through the laborious process of coding in machine language—binary instructions that were as esoteric as they were error-prone. It didn't take long for visionaries to recognize the need for an intermediary, a bridge between human intellect and silicon logic.

Enter the compiler.
The concept of a compiler emerged as a monumental breakthrough, ushering in an era of higher-level programming languages such as Fortran, COBOL, and Lisp. These languages allowed programmers to express their ideas in a more human-readable and intuitive manner. But it was the compiler's role in this grand transformation that truly set the stage for a software revolution.

The Compiler's Mission:
At its core, a compiler is a multifaceted tool with a singular mission: to translate the high-level source code,

written in languages like C++, Java, or Python, into low-level machine code that a computer's central processing unit (CPU) can execute. It is the translator of dreams into reality, the embodiment of creativity distilled into pure functionality.

Imagine for a moment the act of writing code in a high-level language. The words, symbols, and structures flow from the programmer's mind onto the screen, embodying their vision of a software solution. Yet, to transform this conceptual masterpiece into a tangible, executable program, one must invoke the compiler. It serves as the bridge between the abstract and the concrete, transforming lines of elegant code into a binary symphony that powers our digital world.

Compiler Phases:
The journey of a compiler is an intricate one, comprised of several distinct phases, each with its own unique purpose and challenges. In the chapters to come, we will delve deeply into these phases, exploring lexical analysis, syntax parsing, semantic analysis, optimization, and code generation. Each step plays a crucial role in ensuring that the final executable code is not only correct but also efficient.

The Compiler Ecosystem:
Before we conclude our introduction, it is worth mentioning that compilers are not limited to a single programming language or platform. They are versatile tools that have found their place in a wide array of domains. From the compilation of embedded systems firmware to the creation of dynamic web applications, compilers are omnipresent in the modern software development landscape.

Conclusion:

In essence, compilers are the magicians, the linguists, and the engineers of the digital age. They take our ideas and transform them into reality, enabling the digital wonders that define our world. In the pages that follow, we will unravel the inner workings of compilers, gaining insight into their mechanisms, algorithms, and the profound impact they have on software development. So, fasten your seatbelts, for we are about to embark on a journey through the heart of compiler technology, exploring the intricate tapestry that underlies our digital universe.

II. The Structure and Phases of a Typical Compiler

As we embark on our voyage into the realm of compilers, it is crucial to first grasp the intricate structure and the meticulous phases that comprise these digital artisans. A compiler, as it transmutes human-readable source code into machine-executable instructions, is an orchestration of carefully interwoven components, each with a distinct role to play in the grand symphony of software creation.

1. Lexical Analysis:
Imagine the source code as a forest of words and symbols. Before the compiler can decipher their meaning, it must first traverse this wilderness, discerning the boundaries of tokens—the smallest meaningful units of code. This process, known as lexical analysis, involves breaking down the code into a sequence of tokens, stripping away extraneous whitespace and comments. The resulting token stream becomes the foundation upon which the rest of the compiler's work is built.

2. Syntax Parsing:
Having tamed the wild terrain of tokens, the compiler proceeds to the next phase: syntax parsing. Here, it scrutinizes the hierarchical structure of the code,

ensuring that it adheres to the rules of the programming language's grammar. The outcome is an abstract syntax tree (AST), a hierarchical representation that captures the essence of the program's structure, paving the way for deeper analysis.

3. Semantic Analysis:
Once the syntax has been parsed and the AST established, the compiler delves into the realm of semantics. Semantic analysis goes beyond syntax, examining the meaning and correctness of the code. It enforces language-specific rules, checks for variable declarations, type compatibility, and other aspects of program correctness. This phase not only weeds out subtle errors but also paves the way for subsequent optimization.

4. Optimization:
Optimization is the alchemical process wherein the compiler seeks to enhance the code's efficiency and performance. It scrutinizes the program, identifying opportunities for improvement. This can involve anything from constant folding (evaluating expressions at compile-time) to loop unrolling (expanding loops for speed). Optimization is a delicate balance between code size and execution speed, and it varies depending on the compiler and the target platform.

5. Code Generation:
The penultimate phase is code generation, where the compiler crafts the final masterpiece—the machine code. Drawing from the AST and the results of semantic analysis, the compiler generates a sequence of instructions that the computer's CPU can execute. This stage is a meticulous dance of mapping high-level abstractions to low-level machine instructions, a testament to the compiler's ability to translate human intent into binary reality.

6. Output and Execution:
Finally, the compiler assembles the generated machine code into an executable binary file or, in some cases, a virtual machine representation. The output is ready for deployment and execution. At this point, the once-abstract source code has metamorphosed into a tangible software application, breathing life into the digital domain.

Conclusion:
In understanding the structure and phases of a typical compiler, we unravel the inner workings of these remarkable tools. They are not mere translators but orchestrators of creativity, transforming ideas into executable reality. Each phase, from lexical analysis to code generation, represents a crucial step in this journey, where the compiler acts as a bridge between human intelligence and the intricate world of computer logic. In the chapters ahead, we shall explore each of these phases in greater detail, unveiling the magic behind the art of compilation.

III. High-Level Overview of the Compilation Process

In the labyrinthine world of software development, the compiler stands as the unsung hero, a silent architect that transforms the abstract musings of programmers into the concrete realities of executable software. To understand the intricate symphony of compilation, we must first embark on a journey through the high-level overview of the compilation process—a journey that will unveil the magic behind the compiler's transformative power.

1. Source Code: The Composer's Manuscript
Our journey begins with the source code—a meticulously crafted manuscript that embodies the vision of the programmer. This code, written in a high-level

programming language such as C++, Java, or Python, reads like poetry to the human eye, expressing logic, data structures, and algorithms with elegant clarity. It is the composer's masterpiece, filled with purpose and intent.

2. Lexical Analysis: The Code's Grammatical Punctuation

Like a scholar pouring over an ancient text, the compiler's first task is lexical analysis. In this phase, the code is scanned and dissected into tokens—words and symbols that serve as the grammatical punctuation of our programmatic language. Whitespace and comments are stripped away, and the code is broken down into its fundamental building blocks.

3. Syntax Parsing: Constructing the Grammatical Structure

With the tokens in hand, the compiler proceeds to syntax parsing—a process akin to constructing the grammatical structure of a sentence. It analyzes the sequence and arrangement of tokens to determine if they adhere to the rules of the programming language's grammar. The result is an abstract syntax tree (AST), a hierarchical representation that captures the essence of the code's structure.

4. Semantic Analysis: The Code's Semantical Harmony

Beyond syntax lies semantics, where the compiler delves into the meaning and coherence of the code. It ensures that variables are declared before use, that types match correctly, and that the code adheres to the language's semantics. This phase enforces the rules that govern the language and helps catch subtle errors that may not be apparent from syntax alone.

5. Optimization: The Composer's Refinement

Just as a composer revises and refines their musical composition, the compiler engages in optimization. It seeks opportunities to enhance the code's efficiency and performance. This can include simplifying expressions, removing redundancy, or even reordering instructions to reduce execution time. Optimization is a delicate balance between code size and execution speed, where the compiler strives to create the most efficient rendition of the composer's vision.

6. Code Generation: The Masterpiece's Performance

Code generation is where the compiler transmutes the abstract code into the tangible—machine code that a computer's CPU can understand and execute. Drawing from the AST and the results of semantic analysis and optimization, the compiler generates a sequence of low-level instructions. This phase is where the code's performance and behavior are solidified, and the executable program takes shape.

7. Output and Execution: The Grand Performance

Finally, the compiler assembles the generated machine code into an executable binary or bytecode file. This output is ready for deployment and execution on a computer or a virtual machine. The once-abstract source code has now become a tangible software application, ready to perform its intended function.

In this high-level overview of the compilation process, we have glimpsed the compiler's transformative power—a power that takes the programmer's manuscript and transmutes it into the executable masterpiece. As we delve deeper into the subsequent chapters, we will explore each phase of compilation in intricate detail, revealing the intricate machinery that powers the magic of compilers.

IV. Historical Development of Compilers and Their Importance in Modern Computing

To understand the significance of compilers in the modern computing landscape, we must first embark on a journey through time, tracing the historical evolution of these remarkable tools. In doing so, we shall uncover the profound impact they have had on the very essence of software development and the way we interact with the digital world today.

The Dawn of Computing: Pre-Compiler Era

Our story begins in the early days of computing when programmers had no luxury of high-level programming languages. Instead, they had to converse with the machines in the cryptic language of binary code, using arcane assembly languages for a modicum of abstraction. This process was not only error-prone but also exceptionally time-consuming, severely limiting the progress of software development.

The Birth of Fortran: The First High-Level Language

The turning point in this historical narrative occurred in 1957 when IBM unveiled the Fortran (short for Formula Translation) compiler. Developed by a team led by John Backus, this pioneering compiler ushered in a new era. It introduced the concept of high-level programming languages, allowing programmers to write code in a more human-readable form. Fortran's advent marked the dawn of compilers as we know them today.

Explosion of High-Level Languages: The Compiler Renaissance

Following Fortran's success, a flurry of high-level programming languages emerged, each with its own compiler. COBOL, LISP, ALGOL, and many others graced the computing landscape, each designed to cater to specific domains and problem-solving paradigms. Compilers became the enabling force behind this explosion of languages, democratizing software development and fostering innovation.

C and Unix: The Compiler-Driven Revolution
The 1970s witnessed a monumental shift with the development of the C programming language by Dennis Ritchie at Bell Labs. Coupled with the Unix operating system, C not only introduced powerful abstractions but also set the stage for the modern compiler ecosystem. The C compiler, the precursor to GCC (GNU Compiler Collection), became a benchmark for compiler design and optimization.

The Importance of Compilers Today
Fast forward to the present day, and compilers have grown into indispensable tools that shape the very foundations of modern computing. Here's why they are more crucial than ever:

1. High-Level Abstraction: Compilers allow programmers to express complex algorithms and logic in a readable, high-level language, enhancing productivity and reducing error rates.

2. Portability: They bridge the gap between diverse hardware architectures, enabling software to run on various platforms with minimal modifications.

3. Optimization: Compilers employ sophisticated optimization techniques to produce highly efficient machine code, maximizing program performance.

4. Safety: They enforce type checking and other semantic rules, catching errors before runtime, which is critical for robust and secure software.

5. Innovation: The existence of compilers encourages the creation of new programming languages, each

tailored to specific domains, expanding the horizons of software development.

In conclusion, compilers have journeyed from the early days of binary coding to become the backbone of modern computing. Their historical development has been marked by milestones that have not only simplified software development but have also enabled the creation of sophisticated software systems that power our interconnected digital world. In the chapters to come, we will delve deeper into the inner workings of compilers, unveiling the mechanisms and principles that drive their transformative capabilities.

V. Types of Programming Languages and Their Relationship with Compilers

Programming languages are the poets' ink, the artists' canvas, and the architects' blueprints in the world of software creation. They provide the means for humans to communicate their intentions to machines. Yet, the intricate relationship between programming languages and compilers is what breathes life into this communication, defining the very essence of how software is conceived, constructed, and executed.

Low-Level Languages: The Foundation of Computation At the foundation of the programming language spectrum lie low-level languages. These languages, such as Assembly and machine code, are intimately tied to the hardware architecture of computers. They offer programmers unparalleled control over the hardware, allowing them to write instructions that map directly to the CPU's operations. However, this level of control comes at a cost: low-level languages are highly complex, tedious, and error-prone.

Compilers for low-level languages, such as the assembler, serve as a direct translator. They take the human-readable mnemonics of Assembly language and convert them into the binary machine code that the computer's CPU can execute. These compilers focus on the meticulous mapping of instructions, aiming for maximum efficiency in code execution.

High-Level Languages: Bridging the Gap
High-level languages, in stark contrast, prioritize human readability and abstraction. They provide programmers with powerful constructs, data structures, and libraries that simplify the software development process. Languages like Python, Java, and C++ belong to this category, and they have become the lingua franca of modern programming.

The role of a compiler in the context of high-level languages is far more intricate than its low-level counterpart. Here, compilers must perform a multifaceted translation, encompassing several phases:

1. Lexical Analysis and Tokenization: The compiler must break down the high-level code into tokens, identifying keywords, operators, and symbols. This initial parsing sets the stage for subsequent analysis.

2. Syntax Parsing and Abstract Syntax Trees: The compiler analyzes the structure of the code, ensuring it adheres to the language's grammar rules. It constructs an abstract syntax tree (AST) that captures the hierarchical structure of the code.

3. Semantic Analysis: Going beyond syntax, the compiler scrutinizes the meaning and correctness of the code. It enforces type checking, variable scoping rules, and other semantic constraints.

4. Optimization: High-level language compilers engage in a complex process of optimizing the code for

execution speed and efficiency. This involves a variety of techniques, such as constant folding, loop optimization, and function inlining.

5. Code Generation: The heart of the compiler, this phase translates the high-level code into low-level machine code. It maps high-level abstractions to low-level CPU instructions, ensuring that the program performs as intended.

6. Output and Execution: Finally, the compiler produces an executable binary or bytecode file that can be run on a computer or a virtual machine. The high-level code, through the compiler's transformation, becomes a tangible software application.

The relationship between high-level programming languages and compilers is symbiotic. While languages empower programmers with expressive tools, compilers, in turn, enable these languages to transcend the realm of human comprehension, translating them into the realm of digital execution.

In this dynamic interplay between languages and compilers, the possibilities of software development are boundless. As we explore the depths of compiler technology in the chapters to come, we shall gain a deeper appreciation for the intricate synergy that underlies this creative partnership.

Chapter 2: Lexical Analysis

I. Lexical Analysis or Scanning Phase
The First Step in the Compiler's Dance
In the intricate choreography of a compiler, the lexical analysis, often referred to as the scanning phase, takes center stage as the inaugural step in the process. This phase resembles the meticulous scanning of a text by a vigilant librarian, breaking down the source code into its fundamental building blocks – tokens. Tokens are the lexical units that form the foundation upon which the entire compilation process rests.

The Role of Lexical Analysis:
Picture the source code as a vast forest of characters and symbols, an entanglement of words and punctuation. The compiler's first task is to bring order to this wilderness. Lexical analysis serves as the code's grammarian, its sentinel, and its classifier. It reads the code character by character, discerning the spaces between words and sentences, the punctuation that marks boundaries, and the symbols that denote structure.

Scanning the Source Code:
The process begins with a stream of characters, the raw source code. The lexical analyzer dissects this stream, segmenting it into discrete tokens. It identifies keywords, operators, literals, identifiers, and punctuation marks, recognizing the distinct role each plays in the language's grammar. Consider a simple statement in a programming language:

```python
sum = num1 + num2
```

The lexical analyzer, in this case, would identify the following tokens:

1. `sum` (as an identifier)
2. `=` (as an operator)
3. `num1` (as an identifier)
4. `+` (as an operator)
5. `num2` (as an identifier)

Handling Whitespace and Comments:
As the code is scanned, the lexical analyzer disregards superfluous whitespace and comments, ensuring that only meaningful tokens are retained. Whitespace and comments, though essential for human readability, are irrelevant to the compiler's understanding of the code's structure.

Error Handling:
During the scanning phase, the lexical analyzer may also detect errors, such as malformed tokens or unrecognized characters. Error handling is an essential aspect of this process, as it helps catch syntax errors early in the compilation process, providing programmers with valuable feedback.

Building a Token Stream:
Once the scanning is complete, the lexical analyzer produces a stream of tokens that serves as the foundation for subsequent phases of the compiler, such as syntax parsing and semantic analysis. This stream is, in essence, a structured representation of the code, preserving its essential components while abstracting away the details of character-by-character processing.

Language Variations:
It's worth noting that the lexical analysis phase is highly language-dependent. Different programming languages have distinct rules for tokenization. For instance, in C++,

`++` is a valid token representing the increment operator, whereas in Python, `++` would be treated as two separate `+` operators. Therefore, lexical analyzers are tailored to the specific syntax and grammar of the language they are designed to compile.

In the grand orchestration of compiling, lexical analysis is the initial crescendo, where the compiler's journey begins. It lays the groundwork for subsequent phases, shaping the code into a format that can be comprehended by the compiler's intricate machinery. As we delve deeper into the realms of syntax parsing, semantic analysis, and optimization, we shall recognize the indispensable role that lexical analysis plays in the compiler's symphony of code transformation.

II. Tokenization and Regular Expressions
The Art of Language Recognition
As the curtain rises on the lexical analysis phase, one of the key acts in the compiler's theatrical performance, it is essential to delve into the heart of this process: tokenization. Tokenization is akin to parsing sentences in a spoken language, but instead, it deciphers the language of programming, breaking down the source code into its atomic elements – tokens. To accomplish this feat, compilers employ a powerful tool known as regular expressions, a language within a language.

Tokens: The Building Blocks of Code
In the world of programming languages, tokens are the elemental components that give structure and meaning to the code. These tokens come in various forms, encompassing keywords, identifiers, literals, operators, and punctuation marks. They are the words, punctuation, and syntax rules that make up the vocabulary of a programming language.

Consider the following line of code in Python:

```python
result = num1 + num2
```

In this code, the tokens are:

1. `result` (an identifier)
2. `=` (an operator)
3. `num1` (an identifier)
4. `+` (an operator)
5. `num2` (an identifier)

Regular Expressions: The Lexical Analyzer's Toolkit
At the heart of tokenization lies the art of pattern matching, and this is where regular expressions come into play. Regular expressions are a powerful and expressive tool for defining patterns in strings. They act as a universal translator between the free-form nature of human-readable source code and the structured world of tokens.

For example, consider the task of identifying integers in the source code. Regular expressions can be employed to recognize patterns of digits that form integer literals. In Python, the regular expression `\d+` can be used to match one or more digits.

Regular expressions allow the lexical analyzer to define the rules that govern the recognition of tokens. These rules are typically specified in a formal grammar known as a lexical specification, or lexer specification. The lexer specification is language-dependent and outlines the regular expressions that correspond to each type of token in the language.

The Tokenization Process:

When the lexical analyzer encounters the source code, it reads it character by character, attempting to match the regular expressions defined in the lexer specification. As soon as a match is found, a token is generated and added to the stream of tokens. If no match is found, the lexical analyzer continues scanning until a match is identified or an error is detected.

Consider the regular expression for recognizing integers (`\d+`). When the lexical analyzer encounters the characters `12345`, it recognizes them as a sequence of digits and generates the token `12345` with the type "integer literal."

Handling Ambiguities:
While regular expressions are powerful, they can also introduce ambiguities. For instance, consider a programming language where both `+` and `++` are valid tokens. The regular expression for `+` (`\+`) could match both `+` and `++`, leading to ambiguity. To resolve such issues, the lexical analyzer often employs a strategy known as maximal munch, which chooses the longest matching token.

Conclusion:
Tokenization and regular expressions are the first acts in the grand performance of lexical analysis. They are the foundational steps that transform the abstract code into tangible tokens, setting the stage for the subsequent phases of the compiler's dance. In the chapters to come, we shall explore the intricacies of these processes in greater detail, unraveling the techniques and strategies that make lexical analysis a fundamental component of the compiler's artistic repertoire.

III. Finite Automata and Regular Languages
The Elegant Dance of Language Recognition

As we delve deeper into the fascinating world of lexical analysis, we encounter two key players in this intricate ballet: finite automata and regular languages. These concepts, while seemingly abstract, underpin the core mechanisms of token recognition within compilers. They are the choreographers, guiding the lexical analyzer's steps as it transforms raw source code into structured tokens.

Finite Automata: The Dancers of Computation
At the heart of this dance are finite automata—mathematical models of computation that serve as the backbone of lexical analysis. Finite automata, also known as state machines, come in two flavors: deterministic finite automata (DFA) and nondeterministic finite automata (NFA).

Deterministic Finite Automata (DFA): These are elegant, precise machines that follow a predetermined set of rules. A DFA transitions from one state to another based on the input it receives. Each state represents a unique recognition pattern, and the transitions define how the automaton moves from one pattern to the next.

Consider a simple DFA designed to recognize binary integers. It starts in an initial state and processes each digit of the binary number. If it reaches an accepting state at the end, it signals successful recognition.

Nondeterministic Finite Automata (NFA): NFAs, on the other hand, possess a degree of uncertainty. They can transition to multiple states simultaneously based on the same input. This non-determinism allows for more flexibility in recognizing patterns but can also make them more complex to work with.

Regular Languages: The Dance Steps

Regular languages are the choreographed sequences of symbols and patterns that finite automata are designed to recognize. These languages are described by regular expressions—a concise and expressive notation for defining patterns in strings. A regular expression is a sequence of characters and special symbols that represents a set of strings.

For example, the regular expression `\d+` defines a pattern for recognizing one or more digits. It's a fundamental tool in lexical analysis for recognizing integer literals in source code.

Regular languages are closed under various operations, such as union, concatenation, and Kleene closure. This closure property allows regular expressions to define complex patterns in a highly modular and readable manner.

Token Recognition: The Choreography
The choreography of token recognition begins when the lexical analyzer processes the source code character by character. At each step, it consults the finite automata and regular expressions defined in the lexer specification. These automata and expressions guide the analyzer in recognizing the patterns of tokens within the code.

For instance, if the lexer specification defines a regular expression for identifiers `[a-zA-Z_][a-zA-Z0-9_]*`, the analyzer will recognize sequences of letters, digits, and underscores as valid identifiers in the source code.

Conclusion:
Finite automata and regular languages are the graceful dancers in the lexical analysis phase of compilation. They provide a structured framework for recognizing tokens within the seemingly chaotic landscape of source

code. As we delve deeper into the intricacies of lexical analysis, we shall explore the artistry of these tools, understanding how they transform code into a well-structured sequence of tokens, setting the stage for the subsequent acts in the compiler's symphonic performance.

IV. Construction of a Lexer Using Tools Like Lex or Flex

The Art of Automated Tokenization
In the grand production of lexical analysis, building a lexer is a pivotal act. It's the conductor's baton, guiding the orchestra of characters in the source code towards harmonious tokenization. While one could write a lexer from scratch, there's a powerful tool that has taken center stage in this endeavor: Lex, or its open-source counterpart, Flex.

Lexical Analysis: The Prelude
Before we delve into the world of Lex and Flex, it's crucial to understand the role of a lexer in the compiler's symphony. A lexer, short for lexical analyzer, is responsible for breaking down the source code into meaningful tokens. These tokens are the building blocks of the code, each representing an essential element like keywords, identifiers, literals, or punctuation.

Consider a programming language with the following code snippet:

```c
int result = 42;
```

A lexer's task is to recognize and produce the following tokens:

1. `int` (keyword)

2. `result` (identifier)
3. `=` (operator)
4. `42` (integer literal)
5. `;` (punctuation)

The Lexical Analysis Phase:
The process of creating a lexer can be quite intricate, particularly for languages with complex syntax and rich vocabularies. This is where tools like Lex and Flex come to the rescue.

Lex and Flex: The Composer's Quill
Lex and Flex are lexer generator tools that empower compiler developers to define tokenization rules concisely and efficiently. They do this by allowing developers to specify patterns using regular expressions and associate actions with those patterns. This approach allows for the automated generation of a lexer, saving time and reducing the potential for human error.

Here's how the process unfolds:

1. Specification of Token Patterns: In Lex or Flex, you start by defining regular expressions that describe the patterns of tokens in your language. For example, to recognize integers, you might specify a pattern like `\d+`, which matches one or more digits.

2. Associated Actions: Alongside these patterns, you specify actions that should be performed when a particular pattern is matched. Actions can involve generating tokens, capturing the matched text, and performing additional processing as needed.

3. Lexer Generation: Once the patterns and actions are defined, Lex or Flex generates the lexer's C code. This code, when compiled, becomes the heart of the lexer—a

program that can scan the source code and produce a stream of tokens.

4. Integration with the Compiler: The generated lexer can be seamlessly integrated into the compiler's lexical analysis phase, where it takes raw source code as input and produces a stream of tokens that are then used for further processing.

Advantages of Lex and Flex:
Using Lex or Flex offers several advantages in the construction of a lexer:

1. Efficiency: Lexers generated by these tools are highly efficient, making the tokenization process swift even for large codebases.

2. Maintainability: The separation of tokenization rules and actions from the codebase ensures cleaner and more maintainable compiler code.

3. Consistency: Automated lexer generation reduces the risk of errors in tokenization rules, ensuring that the lexer adheres precisely to the language specification.

4. Portability: Lex and Flex-generated lexers can be compiled on various platforms, enhancing the portability of the compiler.

Conclusion:
In the realm of compiler construction, the use of tools like Lex and Flex to build lexers is akin to employing a masterful composer's quill. They empower compiler developers to efficiently and accurately transform source code into a structured stream of tokens, setting the stage for the subsequent acts in the compiler's grand performance. As we journey further into the world of lexical analysis, we shall explore the nuances of lexer

construction, gaining a deeper appreciation for the elegance and efficiency these tools bring to the art of automated tokenization.

V. Error Handling in Lexical Analysis
The Safety Net of Language Recognition
In the intricate dance of lexical analysis, where the choreography involves recognizing and categorizing tokens in the source code, there is an equally vital partner that often goes unnoticed—the safety net of error handling. Just as in any performance, unexpected errors can disrupt the flow, and the role of error handling in lexical analysis is to gracefully address these disruptions while maintaining the integrity of the lexer's performance.

The Imperfect Nature of Source Code:
Source code, like any human creation, is inherently prone to imperfections. A misplaced character, a mistyped keyword, or a syntax error can turn an otherwise graceful code composition into a cacophonous disruption. Therefore, robust error handling is not a mere option but an essential component of a lexer's repertoire.

Types of Errors in Lexical Analysis:
Errors in lexical analysis can manifest in various forms, including:

1. Syntax Errors: These errors occur when the lexer encounters a sequence of characters that does not conform to the language's syntax rules. For instance, missing parentheses in a function call or an incomplete string literal can trigger syntax errors.

2. Unexpected Characters: Sometimes, the lexer encounters characters or symbols that are not part of any valid token in the language. These unexpected characters can disrupt the tokenization process.

3. Ambiguities: Ambiguities arise when the lexer is unsure about how to tokenize a particular sequence of characters. For example, in some languages, the `++` symbol can represent both an increment operator and two consecutive `+` operators, creating ambiguity.

4. Malformed Tokens: Errors can also occur when the lexer attempts to create a token from a sequence of characters that don't match any defined token pattern. This can happen when characters are incorrectly combined.

Handling Errors Gracefully:
The lexer's role in error handling is to detect and report these errors while minimizing disruption to the compilation process. Here are some strategies employed in error handling:

1. Error Reporting: When an error is detected, the lexer generates an error message that provides information about the nature and location of the error. This message is often directed to the compiler's error output stream.

2. Recovery Mechanisms: Depending on the severity of the error, the lexer may attempt to recover and continue tokenization. For example, if it encounters an unexpected character, it can skip that character and continue scanning.

3. Tokenization Continuation: In some cases, rather than abruptly stopping, the lexer may attempt to create a token from a sequence of characters even when an error is detected. This allows the compiler to capture and report the error while still making some progress in tokenization.

4. Error Tokens: Some lexers introduce the concept of "error tokens." These are special tokens created when an error is encountered, allowing the compiler to track and report errors while maintaining tokenization progress.

Improving User Experience:
Effective error handling in lexical analysis is not only about technical correctness but also about providing a positive user experience. The error messages should be informative and actionable, helping programmers understand and correct their mistakes efficiently.

Conclusion:
Error handling in lexical analysis is the safety net that ensures the graceful continuation of the lexer's performance, even in the face of unexpected disruptions. It is an essential component of any compiler's repertoire, improving the robustness and user-friendliness of the compilation process. As we progress through the chapters, we shall continue to explore the strategies and techniques that make error handling in compilers a vital part of the software development symphony.

VI. Examples of Common Lexemes and Tokens
The Vocabulary of Source Code
In the realm of lexical analysis, source code is a language—a language composed not of prose and poetry, but of lexemes and tokens. Lexemes are the individual units of meaning, akin to words in natural language, while tokens are the concrete instances of lexemes found in the source code. In this section, we'll explore a lexicon of common lexemes and tokens that form the vocabulary of source code across various programming languages.

1. Keywords:

Keywords are the reserved words in a programming language that have special meanings and are used to define the structure and logic of programs. Examples include:

- C++: `if`, `while`, `class`, `return`
- Python: `if`, `while`, `def`, `return`
- Java: `if`, `while`, `class`, `return`

In these examples, the keywords serve as lexemes, and each occurrence of a keyword in the source code is a token.

2. Identifiers:
Identifiers are user-defined names for variables, functions, classes, and other program entities. They often follow specific naming conventions, such as using letters, digits, and underscores. Examples include:

- `counter`
- `calculate_total`
- `EmployeeRecord`

Each unique identifier is a lexeme, and each instance of an identifier in the source code is a token.

3. Constants:
Constants are fixed values in the code that don't change during program execution. They can be numeric or string values. Examples include:

- Numeric Constants:
  - `42`
  - `3.141592`
- String Constants:
  - `"Hello, World!"`
  - `"123"`

Numeric and string constants are lexemes, and each instance in the source code is a token.

4. Operators:
Operators are symbols or keywords that perform operations on operands. Examples include:

- Arithmetic Operators:
  - `+`, `-`, `*`, `/`, `%`
- Comparison Operators:
  - `==`, `!=`, `<`, `>`
- Logical Operators:
  - `&&`, `||`, `!`

Operators are both lexemes and tokens, and each occurrence of an operator in the source code is a token.

5. Punctuation:
Punctuation marks are used to separate code elements, control flow, or define structure. Examples include:

- `;` (semicolon) - Used to terminate statements.
- `,` (comma) - Used to separate elements in lists.
- `()` (parentheses) - Used for function calls and grouping expressions.

Punctuation marks are also lexemes and tokens, with each instance serving as a token in the source code.

6. Comments:
Comments are not tokens but are crucial for code documentation and readability. They provide explanations and context for the code. Examples include:

- Single-line comments:
  - `// This is a single-line comment`
- Multi-line comments:

- `` `/* This is a` ``
- `` ` multi-line comment */` ``

Comments are recognized by the lexer but are typically ignored in subsequent phases of compilation.

These examples illustrate the rich lexicon of lexemes and tokens that form the vocabulary of source code. The lexer's role is to recognize and categorize these lexemes, transforming the raw code into a structured sequence of tokens that serve as the foundation for further analysis and compilation. As we continue our exploration of lexical analysis, we'll delve deeper into the intricacies of recognizing and handling these lexemes and tokens in the context of various programming languages.

Chapter 3: Syntax Analysis (Parsing)

I. Syntax Analysis or Parsing Phase

The Architectural Blueprint of Code Structure
In the grand design of a compiler, the syntax analysis phase, often referred to as parsing, occupies a role akin to that of an architect. Just as an architect lays the foundation and designs the structure of a building, the parser defines the structural blueprint of a program from its source code. Parsing is where the abstract syntax of a programming language is brought to life—a process that resembles the transformation of a raw manuscript into a meticulously structured novel.

The Role of Syntax Analysis:
At its core, syntax analysis is responsible for ensuring that the source code adheres to the syntactical rules and grammar of the programming language. It accomplishes this by taking the stream of tokens produced during lexical analysis and organizing them into a hierarchical structure known as the abstract syntax tree (AST). The AST captures the code's syntactical relationships, making it comprehensible to the subsequent phases of the compiler.

Understanding Context-Free Grammars:
The foundation of parsing lies in context-free grammars (CFGs), which serve as the formal rules that govern the syntax of a programming language. A CFG consists of a set of production rules that define how valid program constructs can be formed. These rules are expressed in a notation called Backus-Naur Form (BNF) or Extended Backus-Naur Form (EBNF).

For example, a simplified CFG rule for an assignment statement in a programming language might look like this in EBNF:

```
assignment_statement ::= identifier '=' expression ';'
```

This rule specifies that an assignment statement is composed of an identifier, an equal sign, an expression, and a semicolon.

Top-Down vs. Bottom-Up Parsing:
The parsing process can be approached in two main ways: top-down parsing and bottom-up parsing.

- Top-Down Parsing: This approach starts with the highest-level construct and works its way down to the individual tokens. It is often associated with recursive descent parsing, where each non-terminal symbol in the CFG corresponds to a parsing function.

- Bottom-Up Parsing: In contrast, bottom-up parsing begins with the individual tokens and builds up the hierarchical structure, reducing them to higher-level constructs. LR parsing is a common method used for bottom-up parsing.

Abstract Syntax Trees (AST):
Once the parser successfully constructs the hierarchical structure of the program according to the CFG, it creates an abstract syntax tree (AST). The AST represents the program's syntactic structure in a more abstract and structured form, making it easier for subsequent phases of the compiler, such as semantic analysis and code generation, to operate on the code.

Error Handling in Parsing:
Just as in lexical analysis, parsing must deal with errors gracefully. Syntax errors occur when the code violates the language's grammatical rules. When an error is detected, the parser generates an error message that

provides information about the nature and location of the error. Some parsers attempt to recover from errors and continue parsing to identify multiple errors in a single pass.

Conclusion:
In the grand scheme of compiling, the syntax analysis or parsing phase is the architect's desk where the code's structural blueprint is meticulously designed and organized. It is the phase where the code transitions from a linear sequence of tokens to a hierarchical representation that mirrors the language's abstract syntax. As we delve deeper into parsing in the chapters to come, we will explore the intricacies of different parsing techniques, error handling strategies, and the significance of the abstract syntax tree in the compilation process.

II. Context-Free Grammars and BNF Notation
The Grammar of Code Structure
In the world of compilers, parsing is the act of understanding and organizing the structure of code. At the heart of parsing lies the grammar of the programming language, a set of rules that dictate how code should be structured and how different language constructs relate to one another. Context-free grammars (CFGs) and their notation, often expressed in Backus-Naur Form (BNF), serve as the architects of this grammar, shaping the syntax of programming languages with precision.

Context-Free Grammars (CFGs):
Context-free grammars are a mathematical construct devised by Noam Chomsky in the mid-20th century to formally describe the syntax of programming languages. They are used to define the hierarchical structure of valid programs and are a fundamental component of the parsing process.

A CFG consists of four components:
1. A set of terminal symbols: These are the basic symbols or tokens that appear in the source code. Terminal symbols represent actual keywords, identifiers, operators, and other language elements.

2. A set of non-terminal symbols: These symbols are placeholders that represent groups of related language constructs or substructures. Non-terminals serve as variables in the grammar.

3. A set of production rules: Production rules define how non-terminals can be replaced by a sequence of terminals and non-terminals. Each production rule specifies a syntactic pattern that is valid in the language.

4. A start symbol: This is a designated non-terminal symbol from which the parsing process begins.

Backus-Naur Form (BNF) Notation:
BNF notation is a concise and expressive way to represent context-free grammars. It was developed by John Backus and Peter Naur and has become a standard notation for describing the syntax of programming languages.

In BNF, production rules are defined using the following symbols and conventions:

- `::=` (read as "is defined as"): This symbol separates the non-terminal on the left-hand side from the sequence of terminals and non-terminals on the right-hand side.

- `< >`: Angle brackets enclose non-terminal symbols. For example, `<expression>` represents a non-terminal symbol for expressions.

- `|` (pipe): This symbol represents a choice between alternatives. For example, `<expression> ::= <term> | <term> '+' <expression>` defines two alternative ways to construct an expression.

- Square brackets `[ ]`: Square brackets denote optional elements. For example, `[<optional_parameter>]` means that `<optional_parameter>` may or may not appear.

- Curly braces `{ }`: Curly braces indicate repetition of elements zero or more times. For example, `<list_of_arguments> ::= <expression> {',' <expression>}` defines a comma-separated list of expressions.

Example CFG in BNF:
Let's illustrate CFG and BNF notation with a simple rule for an if statement in a hypothetical programming language:

```bnf
<if_statement> ::= 'if' '(' <expression> ')' '{' <statements>
'}' ['else' '{' <statements> '}']
```

In this BNF rule:

- `<if_statement>` is a non-terminal symbol representing if statements.
- `if`, `(`, `)`, `{`, and `}` are terminal symbols.
- `<expression>` and `<statements>` are non-terminal symbols representing expressions and statements, respectively.
- The rule specifies the syntax for an if statement, including optional "else" clauses.

Conclusion:
Context-free grammars and BNF notation are the architects of code structure, defining the syntactical rules

that govern programming languages. They serve as the blueprint for parsers, enabling compilers to understand and organize the hierarchical structure of code. In the chapters ahead, we will explore how parsers use these grammars and notations to build abstract syntax trees, transforming raw code into structured representations ready for further analysis and compilation.

III. Top-Down vs. Bottom-Up Parsing Techniques

The Art of Language Interpretation
In the realm of syntax analysis, parsing is the interpreter's role, deciphering the intricate structure of code and making sense of its syntactic intricacies. Two fundamental approaches guide this interpretive dance: top-down parsing and bottom-up parsing. Each approach brings its own set of techniques and trade-offs to the stage, enriching the repertoire of compiler design.

Top-Down Parsing: The Producer's Perspective
Imagine a director guiding actors through a script, starting with the overarching storyline and gradually drilling down to individual lines and actions. This directorial approach is analogous to top-down parsing, where the parser begins with the highest-level construct and recursively expands its focus to the details.

Recursive Descent Parsing:
One of the most prevalent top-down parsing techniques is recursive descent parsing. In this approach, the parser employs a set of recursive procedures, each dedicated to recognizing a specific non-terminal symbol in the grammar. These procedures correspond directly to the non-terminals in the context-free grammar (CFG).

Consider the following simplified CFG rule:

```
```

<expression> ::= <term> '+' <expression>

```
```

In a recursive descent parser, there would be a parsing procedure for `<expression>`, which calls procedures for `<term>` and `<expression>` to recognize the parts of the expression and their relationship. This recursive structure mirrors the nested nature of expressions in programming languages.

Predictive Parsing:
Predictive parsing is a specialized form of top-down parsing where the parser predicts which production rule to apply based on the next few tokens in the input stream. It uses a parsing table, often implemented as a parsing table or a predictive parsing table, to make these predictions. Predictive parsers are efficient and capable of handling LL(k) grammars, where "LL" stands for "left-to-right, leftmost derivation" and "k" represents the number of lookahead tokens.

Advantages of Top-Down Parsing:
- Readability: Recursive descent parsers can be implemented in a way that closely mirrors the structure of the CFG, making the parser code more readable and maintainable.

- Ease of Error Handling: Top-down parsers are often better at providing meaningful error messages, thanks to their explicit structure.

- Natural for LL Grammars: Top-down parsing techniques align well with LL grammars, which are common in many programming languages.

Bottom-Up Parsing: The Detective's Deduction
In contrast to top-down parsing, bottom-up parsing begins with individual tokens and constructs the higher-

level syntactic structures step by step, like a detective piecing together a complex puzzle from scattered clues.

LR Parsing:
LR (Left-to-right, Rightmost derivation) parsing is a popular bottom-up parsing technique. LR parsers use a parsing table and a stack data structure to systematically reduce sequences of tokens to non-terminals. The "L" denotes scanning input from left to right, while "R" refers to building the rightmost derivation.

LR parsing is capable of handling a broader class of grammars, including many commonly used programming languages. The most famous LR parsing algorithm is the LALR(1) (Look-Ahead, LR with 1-token lookahead) parsing algorithm.

Shift-Reduce Parsing:
In bottom-up parsing, the parser continually shifts input symbols onto the stack until it can reduce a portion of the stack to a non-terminal symbol. This reduction step replaces the right-hand side of a production rule with the corresponding non-terminal, effectively moving from detailed tokens to higher-level constructs.

Advantages of Bottom-Up Parsing:
- Handling Ambiguity: Bottom-up parsing can handle ambiguous grammars and is capable of resolving ambiguities during parsing.

- Wider Range of Grammars: It can handle a broader range of grammars, including those not suited for top-down parsing.

- Efficiency: LR parsing, in particular, is known for its efficiency and ability to generate parsers for large grammars.

Choosing the Right Technique:
The choice between top-down and bottom-up parsing depends on several factors, including the complexity of the language's syntax, the efficiency requirements, and the trade-offs in error handling and maintainability. Many modern compilers employ a combination of parsing techniques to balance these factors and achieve a robust and efficient parsing process.

Conclusion:
Top-down and bottom-up parsing techniques are the directors of the compiler's interpretive performance, each with its unique style and strengths. As we progress through this chapter and beyond, we'll continue to explore the intricacies of parsing, diving deeper into the techniques and tools that make parsing a crucial component of the compilation process.

IV. LL(1) and LR(1) Parsing

The Precision Tools of Syntax Analysis
In the intricate landscape of parsing, where code structure is scrutinized and hierarchically organized, two powerful parsing techniques emerge as stalwart champions: LL(1) and LR(1) parsing. These techniques are like precision instruments, capable of navigating complex grammars and deciphering the syntax of programming languages with remarkable accuracy.

LL(1) Parsing: The Look-Ahead Detective
Imagine a detective who can deduce the next move of a criminal by observing just one piece of evidence. LL(1) parsing operates on a similar principle by examining a single token of lookahead to predict the next production rule. It is well-suited for programming languages with relatively simple and unambiguous syntax.

Key Features of LL(1) Parsing:

1. Left-to-Right Scanning: LL(1) parsing reads the input from left to right, in the order it appears in the source code. This is a natural reading direction for many programming languages.

2. Leftmost Derivation: The LL(1) parser constructs a leftmost derivation of the input string. This means it builds the parse tree by expanding the leftmost non-terminal at each step.

3. 1-Token Lookahead: The '1' in LL(1) indicates that the parser examines just one token of lookahead to make parsing decisions. This means that the parser considers only the current token when determining which production rule to apply.

LL(1) Parsing Table:
The heart of LL(1) parsing is the LL(1) parsing table. This table is constructed from the grammar's production rules and the first and follow sets for each non-terminal. The first set contains the terminal symbols that can start a string derived from a non-terminal, while the follow set contains the terminal symbols that can follow a string derived from a non-terminal.

Using the parsing table, the LL(1) parser can swiftly determine which production rule to apply based on the current non-terminal and the next token.

Advantages of LL(1) Parsing:
- Efficiency: LL(1) parsers are often more efficient than their LR counterparts because they require only one token of lookahead.

- Readability: LL(1) parsing tables are relatively easy to construct and read, making LL(1) grammars more approachable for humans.

- Error Reporting: LL(1) parsers tend to provide better error messages due to their simpler structure.

LR(1) Parsing: The Grammatical Detective
LR(1) parsing takes a more comprehensive approach, akin to a detective who pieces together a complex puzzle using all available evidence. It is a more powerful and flexible parsing technique capable of handling a broader class of grammars, including those with more complex syntax and ambiguities.

Key Features of LR(1) Parsing:
1. Left-to-Right Scanning: Like LL(1) parsing, LR(1) parsing scans the input from left to right.

2. Rightmost Derivation: An LR(1) parser constructs a rightmost derivation, meaning it expands the rightmost non-terminal at each step while building the parse tree.

3. 1-Token Lookahead: LR(1) parsing also uses a single token of lookahead to make parsing decisions, but unlike LL(1), it considers the next token as well as the current one.

LR(1) Parsing Table:
The core of LR(1) parsing is the LR(1) parsing table. Constructing this table is a more involved process than creating an LL(1) table. The LR(1) parsing table handles the complexities of the parsing process by considering both the current and next tokens and their context.

Advantages of LR(1) Parsing:
- Handling Ambiguities: LR(1) parsing can handle grammars with left-recursion, right-recursion, and other complexities that LL(1) parsers may struggle with.

- Broad Applicability: LR(1) parsing is capable of parsing a wider range of grammars, including those that are more ambiguous or context-sensitive.

- Automatic Generation: Tools like Yacc and Bison can automatically generate LR(1) parsers from grammar specifications, reducing the manual effort in parser construction.

Choosing the Right Parsing Technique:
The choice between LL(1) and LR(1) parsing depends on several factors, including the complexity of the language's syntax, the availability of parser generation tools, and the trade-offs in terms of efficiency and error handling. Many modern compilers use LR(1) or variations like LALR(1) parsing due to their flexibility and handling of more complex grammars.

Conclusion:
LL(1) and LR(1) parsing are the precision instruments in the toolkit of syntax analysis, each with its own strengths and areas of expertise. These techniques empower compilers to navigate the intricate structure of code, bringing the syntax of programming languages to life with remarkable accuracy. As we delve deeper into parsing in the chapters ahead, we will explore how these techniques are applied in practice and how they contribute to the successful compilation of diverse programming languages.

V. Construction of a Parser Using Tools like Yacc or Bison
The Art of Automating Parsing
In the grand symphony of compiler construction, parsing is the act of unraveling the intricate tapestry of code syntax, transforming it into a structured representation that can be understood and manipulated. Parsing, though essential, is a complex endeavor. Fortunately,

tools like Yacc (Yet Another Compiler Compiler) and Bison have stepped onto the compiler's stage as virtuoso composers, simplifying the composition of parsers with their automated symphony.

The Role of Parser Generators:
Parser generators like Yacc and Bison are software tools that automate the creation of parsers. They take as input a formal grammar specification, typically written in Backus-Naur Form (BNF) or a similar notation, and generate parser code in a programming language such as C or C++. This code, when compiled, becomes the heart of the parser—a program capable of transforming a stream of tokens into a structured representation, often an abstract syntax tree (AST).

Key Components of a Parser Generator:
The construction of a parser using tools like Yacc or Bison involves several key components:

1. Grammar Specification: The heart of the process is the definition of the grammar for the language being parsed. This grammar is expressed in a formal notation such as BNF or EBNF and serves as the blueprint for the parser.

2. Parser Generator Tool: Yacc and Bison are examples of parser generator tools. They take the grammar specification as input and generate parser code.

3. Lexer Integration: Typically, the parser generator assumes the existence of a lexer, which is responsible for tokenizing the input source code. The lexer provides the parser with a stream of tokens to work with.

4. Parser Code Templates: The parser generator incorporates templates for generating parser code. These templates include sections for defining actions

associated with grammar rules, handling error recovery, and constructing the abstract syntax tree.

The Yacc and Bison Approach:
Yacc and Bison work on the principles of LR parsing, more specifically LALR (Look-Ahead, LR) parsing. This technique enables the parser to consider both the current token and a limited number of lookahead tokens to make parsing decisions.

The typical workflow when using Yacc or Bison is as follows:

1. Grammar Definition: Write the grammar for the language using BNF or a similar notation. Define the syntax rules, associating actions with each rule that specify what to do when that rule is recognized.

2. Parser Generator Execution: Run the Yacc or Bison tool on the grammar specification. The tool generates parser code, typically in C or C++, that is specific to your grammar.

3. Integration with Lexer: Integrate the generated parser code with a lexer. The lexer tokenizes the source code and provides tokens to the parser.

4. Parsing: Use the combined lexer and parser to parse the input source code. The parser recognizes the grammar rules and executes actions as specified in the grammar definition.

5. AST Construction: During parsing, as specified by the actions in the grammar, the parser constructs an abstract syntax tree (AST) that represents the structure of the code. The AST serves as the structured representation of the source code, facilitating subsequent phases of compilation.

Advantages of Yacc and Bison:

1. Efficiency: Parser generators produce efficient parsers that can handle large input files quickly.

2. Automated Error Handling: They often include mechanisms for generating detailed error messages and handling syntax errors gracefully.

3. Maintainability: By separating grammar specification from parser code, these tools promote cleaner and more maintainable codebases.

Conclusion:
Parser generators like Yacc and Bison are virtuoso composers in the compiler's orchestra, automating the intricate process of parsing. They take the grammar specification as their score and, with the help of lexers, transform source code into structured representations. As we journey further into the world of parsing, we will explore the nuances of parser construction, gaining a deeper appreciation for the elegance and efficiency these tools bring to the art of automated code interpretation.

VI. Syntax Tree Generation
The Art of Structured Interpretation
In the intricate choreography of parsing, where code structure is deciphered and organized, syntax tree generation takes center stage. Like a conductor leading a symphony, this phase transforms the raw code into a structured, hierarchical representation, the abstract syntax tree (AST). The syntax tree is the architectural backbone of a compiler, providing a structured interpretation of the code's semantics.

The Purpose of Syntax Trees:

Syntax trees serve as a bridge between the raw source code and the subsequent phases of compilation. They capture the hierarchical structure of the code and its relationships, facilitating error checking, optimization, and code generation. Each node in the tree corresponds to a syntactic construct, such as a statement or an expression, while the edges represent the relationships between these constructs.

Construction of Syntax Trees:
Syntax tree generation typically occurs during the parsing phase of compilation. As the parser processes the input code according to the rules defined in the grammar, it constructs the syntax tree incrementally. The parser is guided by the grammar's production rules and actions associated with those rules.

Example Syntax Tree:
Consider a simple assignment statement in a programming language:

```python
x = y + 42
```

The corresponding syntax tree might look like this:

```
    =
   / \
  x   +
     / \
    y  42
```

In this syntax tree:

- The root node represents the assignment operator (`=`).
- The left child node represents the variable `x`.
- The right child node represents the addition operator (`+`).
- The left child of the addition node represents the variable `y`.
- The right child of the addition node represents the numeric constant `42`.

Each node in the syntax tree corresponds to a specific token or syntactic construct in the source code, and the tree's structure mirrors the hierarchical relationships between these constructs.

Advantages of Syntax Trees:

1. Structured Representation: Syntax trees provide a structured, unambiguous representation of the code's syntax, making it easier for subsequent compiler phases to analyze and manipulate.

2. Semantic Understanding: By capturing the syntax of the code, syntax trees enable the compiler to begin understanding the code's semantics, paving the way for semantic analysis and optimization.

3. Error Detection: Syntax trees facilitate the detection of syntax errors by highlighting inconsistencies or violations of the language's grammar.

Abstract Syntax Trees (AST):
While syntax trees faithfully represent the code's syntactic structure, they often contain more details than necessary. Abstract syntax trees (ASTs) are a refined version of syntax trees, focusing on the essential semantic structure of the code while omitting syntactic details. ASTs strip away elements like parentheses and

redundant nodes, retaining only the constructs that influence the code's meaning.

Example AST:
For the assignment statement mentioned earlier, the corresponding AST might look like this:

```
```
    =
   / \
  x   +
     /\
    y 42
```
```

In this AST, the addition operator `+` and numeric constant `42` are siblings of the assignment operator `=`, indicating that they are part of the same expression.

Conclusion:
Syntax tree generation is the architect's blueprint, transforming the raw code into a structured interpretation that lays the foundation for subsequent phases of compilation. Syntax trees and their abstract counterparts, ASTs, are the linguistic bridge between code and compiler, enabling the analysis, optimization, and transformation of code with precision and clarity. As we continue our journey through the world of compilers, we will explore how these trees evolve and mature, shaping the destiny of programs as they progress through the compilation process.

VII. Handling Syntax Errors
Navigating the Mistakes in Code
In the intricate dance of compiling, where source code is transformed into executable programs, one must address a fundamental challenge: syntax errors. These errors, akin to missed steps in a choreographed

performance, can disrupt the graceful interpretation of code. In this section, we explore the art of gracefully navigating syntax errors during the parsing phase.

The Nature of Syntax Errors:
Syntax errors occur when the code violates the grammar rules of the programming language. These errors can take many forms, including missing semicolons, unmatched parentheses, undefined variables, and more. While syntax errors are common during software development, they present a significant challenge to compilers, which must provide meaningful feedback to programmers.

Error Detection vs. Error Recovery:
Handling syntax errors is a two-fold endeavor. First, the parser must detect the presence of an error in the code. Second, it must decide how to recover from that error and continue parsing. Let's explore each aspect in detail:

Error Detection:

- Locating the Error: The parser detects errors when it encounters unexpected tokens or an incomplete construct that violates the grammar rules. For example, if a semicolon is missing at the end of a statement, the parser detects an error when it encounters the next statement.

- Error Reporting: Once an error is detected, the parser should provide clear and informative error messages. These messages should pinpoint the location of the error and offer suggestions to help the programmer understand and correct the issue.

Error Recovery:

- Resynchronization: Error recovery aims to bring the parser back into a state where it can continue parsing. One common approach is resynchronization, where the parser skips input tokens until it finds a token that allows it to resume parsing. For example, if a semicolon is missing at the end of a statement, the parser might skip tokens until it finds the start of the next statement.

- Partial Parsing: In some cases, the parser may perform a partial parse of the code, identifying as many errors as possible and attempting to recover. This can help programmers identify multiple errors in a single pass.

Example Error Handling:
Consider the following code snippet with a syntax error:

```c
for (int i = 0; i < 10 i++) {
    printf("Hello, World!\n");
}
```

In this code, there's a missing semicolon after the loop condition, and the parser will detect the error. A well-designed compiler would report an error message like:

```
Syntax error: Unexpected token 'i' at line 1, column 21.
Expected ';' after the loop condition.
```

The error message pinpoints the location of the error, identifies the unexpected token ('i'), and provides a suggestion to insert a semicolon.

Challenges and Trade-Offs:
Handling syntax errors can be challenging because:

- Errors can propagate, causing subsequent errors in the code.
- Detecting and recovering from errors without getting stuck in an infinite loop or reporting excessive false positives requires careful design.

Compiler writers must strike a balance between providing helpful error messages and maintaining performance and simplicity.

Conclusion:
Handling syntax errors is an essential aspect of compiler design. A well-implemented error handling mechanism can significantly enhance the user experience by providing clear and actionable feedback to programmers. It allows developers to identify and rectify issues in their code, ultimately contributing to the creation of robust and reliable software. As we continue to explore the intricacies of syntax analysis and parsing, we will delve deeper into the strategies and techniques employed by compilers to gracefully navigate the challenges posed by syntax errors.

Chapter 4: Semantic Analysis

I. Semantic Analysis Phase and Its Importance
The Art of Code Understanding
As we progress through the journey of compiling, we enter the realm of semantic analysis—a phase of profound significance in the compilation process. In this chapter, we explore the essence of semantic analysis, unravel its intricacies, and uncover its vital role in ensuring that code not only compiles but also behaves correctly and meaningfully.

The Essence of Semantic Analysis:
Semantic analysis, often referred to as the "heart" of compilation, goes beyond the syntax of the code. While syntax analysis (parsing) establishes the structure of the program, semantic analysis delves into the meaning and intent behind the code. It is the phase where the compiler seeks to answer fundamental questions such as:

- Does this code adhere to the language's rules and constraints?
- Do the expressions have well-defined types?
- Are variables being used before they are declared?
- Are function calls made with the correct number and types of arguments?

In essence, semantic analysis acts as the bridge between the abstract syntax tree (AST) and the semantic understanding of the code.

The Importance of Semantic Analysis:
Semantic analysis serves several critical purposes, each contributing to the overall reliability and correctness of the compiled code:

1. Error Detection: One of its primary functions is to identify and report semantic errors. These errors may not be apparent from the syntax alone but can lead to unexpected and incorrect program behavior. Examples include type mismatches, undefined variables, and function call mismatches.

2. Type Checking: Semantic analysis enforces type correctness. It ensures that operations and assignments are performed on compatible data types. For instance, it prevents the addition of a string to an integer without explicit conversion.

3. Symbol Resolution: It resolves references to variables, functions, and other symbols in the code. This includes verifying that variables are declared before they are used and that function names match their declarations.

4. Scope Analysis: The compiler tracks variable scopes to ensure that variables are accessed within their valid scopes. This prevents issues like accessing local variables from outside their functions.

5. Memory Management: Some semantic analysis tasks relate to memory management, such as checking for memory leaks and ensuring proper deallocation of resources.

Example of Semantic Analysis:
Consider the following C code snippet:

```c
int x = 5;
int y = "hello";
int z = x + y;
```

Here, semantic analysis would detect several issues:

- A type mismatch when initializing `y` with a string literal.
- An incompatible addition operation between an integer and a string.

A well-designed compiler would produce error messages highlighting these issues:

```

Semantic error: Incompatible types for variable 'y'. Expected 'int', but got 'string'.
Semantic error: Incompatible types in the addition operation. 'int' + 'string'.
```

Challenges in Semantic Analysis:
Semantic analysis is a complex phase with its own set of challenges:

- Complexity of Type Systems: Different programming languages have varying degrees of complexity in their type systems. Some languages are statically typed, while others are dynamically typed, and some have sophisticated type inference systems.

- Scoping and Symbol Resolution: Handling variable scopes, namespaces, and nested declarations can be intricate. Resolving symbols correctly requires careful management of symbol tables.

- Memory Management: Memory analysis and management can be intricate, especially in languages that allow manual memory allocation and deallocation.

- Optimization Opportunities: Semantic analysis presents opportunities for optimization, such as constant folding and dead code elimination.

Conclusion:
Semantic analysis is the compiler's philosopher, deciphering the meaning and intent behind the code. It ensures that the program not only compiles but also behaves correctly and meaningfully. With its ability to detect errors, enforce type correctness, and facilitate correct program behavior, semantic analysis plays a pivotal role in the compilation journey. As we delve deeper into this phase in the chapters ahead, we will uncover the strategies, techniques, and nuances that enable compilers to master the art of code understanding.

II. Static vs. Dynamic Semantics
The Dance of Compile-Time and Run-Time Understanding
In the intricate ballet of programming languages, understanding the semantics of code is essential. The semantics define not just how the code should look but also how it should behave when executed. To understand this behavior, we delve into two fundamental dimensions: static semantics and dynamic semantics.

Static Semantics: The Choreography of Compile-Time
Static semantics, often referred to as compile-time semantics, is the aspect of language interpretation that can be determined by analyzing the code without executing it. It deals with rules and constraints that must be satisfied during the compilation process. The primary goal of static semantics is to ensure that the code adheres to the language's specifications before it is even run.

Key Aspects of Static Semantics:

1. Type Checking: One of the central concerns of static semantics is type checking. It ensures that operations,

expressions, and assignments are performed using compatible data types. For example, it prevents adding a string to an integer or comparing unrelated types.

2. Declaration and Scope Analysis: Static semantics verifies that variables and identifiers are correctly declared before they are used. It also enforces rules related to variable scope, preventing access to undeclared or out-of-scope variables.

3. Function and Procedure Signatures: Static semantics checks that function and procedure calls match their respective declarations in terms of the number and types of arguments and the return type.

4. Memory Management: In some languages, static semantics may include checks related to memory allocation, deallocation, and resource management.

Dynamic Semantics: The Dance of Run-Time Execution Dynamic semantics, also known as run-time semantics, governs the behavior of a program as it executes. It defines how statements and expressions interact with data at run-time, determining the flow of control and the actual computation that occurs during program execution.

Key Aspects of Dynamic Semantics:
1. Execution Order: Dynamic semantics dictates the order in which statements are executed. It defines how control structures like loops and conditionals affect the program's flow.

2. Data Manipulation: It specifies how data is manipulated during execution, including assignments, arithmetic operations, and function calls.

3. Exception Handling: Dynamic semantics defines how the program handles exceptional conditions, such as division by zero or accessing an out-of-bounds array element.

4. Concurrency and Parallelism: In concurrent and parallel programming languages, dynamic semantics describes how multiple threads or processes interact and synchronize.

II. Static vs. Dynamic Semantics
A Synchronized Performance
Static and dynamic semantics complement each other, working together to ensure that code behaves correctly and efficiently:

- Static semantics: Provides compile-time checks and constraints, catching errors before the code is executed. It helps maintain code correctness and robustness.

- Dynamic semantics: Governs the actual behavior of the code at run-time, determining how computations are carried out and how data evolves during execution.

Example Scenario:
Consider a simple C code snippet:

```c
int x = 5;
int y = "hello";
int z = x + y;
```

Static semantics analysis would detect issues like type mismatch during compilation, preventing the code from proceeding to run-time execution with incompatible data types.

Conclusion:
Static and dynamic semantics are the choreographers of code understanding, with static semantics performing the rehearsal before the show and dynamic semantics executing the dance during the performance. Their synchronized performance ensures that code not only compiles successfully but also executes correctly and meaningfully. As we continue our exploration into semantic analysis, we will uncover the strategies, techniques, and nuances that compilers employ to master this intricate dance of compile-time and run-time understanding.

III. Type Checking and Type Inference
The Grammar of Data
In the world of programming languages, data is the language of expression, and type is its grammar. Type checking and type inference are two critical aspects of semantic analysis, serving as the gatekeepers of data correctness and consistency. In this section, we dive into the nuances of type checking and the elegance of type inference.

Type Checking: The Language Grammar Enforcer
Type checking is the process of ensuring that data in a program adheres to a well-defined set of types and follows the language's rules for type interactions. It's the compiler's role as the language grammar enforcer, ensuring that expressions, operations, and assignments are carried out with data of compatible types.

Key Aspects of Type Checking:

1. Type Compatibility: Type checking verifies that operations are performed on operands of compatible types. For example, it ensures that you can't add a string to an integer or compare a boolean to a string.

2. Function Signatures: Type checking enforces that function and method calls match their respective declarations in terms of the number and types of arguments and the return type.

3. Variable Declarations: It confirms that variables are declared with a specific type and that subsequent usage aligns with this type.

4. Type Coercion: In some languages, type checking includes rules for type coercion or implicit type conversion. For instance, converting an integer to a floating-point number for an arithmetic operation.

Example of Type Checking:
Consider the following Python code snippet:

```python
x = 5
y = "hello"
z = x + y
```

In this code, type checking would catch the error in the third line where an integer and a string are being added, as Python does not permit adding these incompatible types. The compiler or interpreter would produce an error message indicating the type mismatch.

Type Inference: The Subtle Grammar Scholar
Type inference is a more subtle aspect of type analysis. It is the process by which the compiler deduces or infers the types of expressions and variables without explicit type declarations. In languages that support type inference, programmers can write code without specifying types explicitly, relying on the compiler to determine them.

Key Aspects of Type Inference:

1. Local Type Deduction: Type inference often applies to variables declared within functions or blocks. The compiler examines the variable's initialization and usage to infer its type.

2. Polymorphism: Type inference can be linked with polymorphism, allowing functions to accept arguments of different types and return values of varying types based on context.

3. Static vs. Dynamic Typing: Some languages, like Haskell and ML, rely heavily on static type inference, ensuring that all types are known at compile-time. In contrast, dynamically typed languages like Python and JavaScript use dynamic typing, inferring types at runtime.

Example of Type Inference:
In the functional programming language Haskell, you can write a function that adds two values without explicitly specifying their types:

```haskell
add x y = x + y
```

The Haskell compiler infers that `x` and `y` should be of numeric types, allowing you to add integers, floating-point numbers, or other numeric types without changing the function.

Challenges and Trade-offs:
Type checking and type inference introduce challenges:

- Complex Type Systems: Some languages have intricate type systems, including generics, type bounds, and user-defined types, which can make type checking and inference more complex.

- Balancing Flexibility and Safety: Languages must strike a balance between providing flexibility through type inference and ensuring safety through type checking. Too much inference can lead to subtle bugs, while strict checking can make code verbose.

- Error Messages: Providing clear and informative error messages is crucial for type-related issues, helping programmers understand and correct their code.

Conclusion:
Type checking and type inference are the grammar scholars of data, ensuring that the language's expressions and operations adhere to a consistent and meaningful structure. They are essential elements of semantic analysis, playing a vital role in both error prevention and efficient code generation. As we continue our exploration of semantic analysis, we will uncover the strategies, techniques, and nuances that compilers employ to master the intricacies of data typing and type analysis.

IV. Symbol Tables and Their Role in Semantic Analysis

The Compiler's Lexicon
In the world of compilers, where source code transforms into executable programs, symbol tables serve as the compiler's lexicon, holding the key to understanding the code's structure and semantics. In this section, we delve into the intricacies of symbol tables and unveil their indispensable role in semantic analysis.

The Significance of Symbol Tables:
Symbol tables are data structures employed by compilers to manage and store information about the

symbols (identifiers, variables, functions, classes, etc.) used within a program. These tables act as a bridge between the code and the compiler, facilitating the interpretation of the code's semantics and ensuring its correctness.

Key Functions of Symbol Tables:

1. Symbol Identification: Symbol tables map identifiers (such as variable and function names) to their associated attributes. These attributes may include data types, memory locations, scope information, and more.

2. Scope Management: They help track the scope of variables, ensuring that identifiers are resolved correctly within their respective scopes. This includes handling issues like shadowing, where a local variable hides a variable with the same name in an outer scope.

3. Type Checking: Symbol tables store type information for variables and functions, allowing the compiler to perform type checking and verification.

4. Declaration and Definition Tracking: Symbol tables keep track of where symbols are declared and where they are defined. This helps the compiler detect issues like using variables before they are declared.

5. Error Detection: They play a crucial role in identifying errors such as undeclared variables, redeclarations, and name clashes.

Components of Symbol Tables:
A symbol table typically consists of the following components:

1. Symbol Name: The identifier or name of the symbol.

2. Data Type: The type associated with the symbol, which may include built-in types, user-defined types, or function signatures.

3. Memory Location: For variables, this could include information about stack or heap allocation. For functions, it may include the address or entry point.

4. Scope Information: Details about the scope in which the symbol is defined, which helps resolve scope-related issues.

5. Attributes: Additional attributes relevant to the symbol, such as array dimensions, function parameters, or visibility modifiers.

Role of Symbol Tables in Semantic Analysis:
Semantic analysis is the phase where the code's semantics are deeply examined and verified. Symbol tables play a pivotal role in this process:

1. Scope Resolution: Symbol tables help determine the scope in which an identifier is used and ensure that the correct symbol is accessed.

2. Type Checking: Type information stored in symbol tables allows the compiler to perform type checks, ensuring that operations are performed on compatible data types.

3. Error Detection: By tracking declarations and definitions, symbol tables aid in identifying errors such as undeclared variables and redeclarations.

4. Optimization: Symbol tables may also be used in optimization techniques like constant folding and dead code elimination.

Example Scenario:
Consider the following C code snippet:

```c
int x = 5;

void foo() {
    int x = 10;
    // ...
}
```

In this code, symbol tables would be used to differentiate between the two variables named `x` in different scopes. The symbol table entries would record their types, scopes, and memory locations, allowing the compiler to resolve variable references correctly.

Challenges and Trade-offs:
Symbol table management presents its own set of challenges:

- Efficiency: Efficient symbol table lookup and management are crucial for compiler performance, especially in large codebases.

- Complexity: Handling complex type systems, scoping rules, and language features can be intricate.

- Error Reporting: Symbol tables must facilitate clear and informative error messages for programmers.

Conclusion:
Symbol tables are the compilers' lexicons, holding the keys to understanding the structure and semantics of code. They are the silent orchestrators of semantic analysis, ensuring that symbols are identified, scopes are managed, types are checked, and errors are

detected. As we delve deeper into the world of semantic analysis, we will uncover the strategies, techniques, and nuances compilers employ to master the art of symbol table management and code interpretation.

V. Attribute Grammars
The Symphony of Code Annotations
In the compiler's symphony, where source code is transformed into an executable masterpiece, attribute grammars play a harmonious role as the composers of annotations and semantics. In this section, we will explore the captivating world of attribute grammars and their vital role in the art of semantic analysis.

The Essence of Attribute Grammars:
Attribute grammars are a formal framework for specifying and calculating attributes associated with the grammar of a programming language. These attributes provide additional information about the structure and semantics of the code. Attribute grammars bridge the gap between the abstract syntax tree (AST) and the rich tapestry of semantics, allowing compilers to annotate and interpret the code's meaning.

Key Aspects of Attribute Grammars:

1. Attributes: Attributes are properties or values associated with elements of the grammar. They can represent a wide range of information, Including data types, symbol names, scope information, type constraints, and more.

2. Grammar Rules: Attribute grammars extend context-free grammars with attributes, associating them with non-terminals (symbols) in the grammar. These attributes can be synthesized attributes, which gather information from child nodes, or inherited attributes,

which pass information from parent nodes to child nodes.

3. Attribute Evaluation: The core of attribute grammars is attribute evaluation, which involves the calculation of attribute values based on the rules defined in the grammar. This process typically occurs during the construction of the AST.

4. Semantic Analysis: Attribute grammars are a powerful tool for semantic analysis, as they allow compilers to verify type correctness, resolve symbols, and enforce language-specific constraints.

Attribute Grammars in Action:
Let's consider a simplified example in a C-like language where attribute grammars help calculate the types of expressions:

```c
int x = 5;
float y = 3.14;
float z = x + y;
```

In this code, attribute grammars can annotate the AST with attribute information for each expression node, such as:

- The variable `x` has an integer type.
- The variable `y` has a float type.
- The addition expression `x + y` has a float type, which is determined by the attribute grammars through type inference rules.

Role of Attribute Grammars in Semantic Analysis:
Attribute grammars play a pivotal role in semantic analysis:

1. Type Checking: They facilitate type inference and type checking by annotating expressions and variables with their data types and ensuring that operations are performed on compatible types.

2. Symbol Resolution: Attribute grammars can help resolve symbols by associating variables and functions with their declarations in symbol tables.

3. Scope Analysis: They enable the tracking of variable scopes and ensure that variables are used within their valid scopes.

4. Error Detection: Attribute grammars can detect semantic errors such as type mismatches, undeclared variables, and incorrect function calls.

5. Optimization: Attribute grammars can aid in optimization by annotating the AST with information that can be used to optimize code generation.

Challenges and Benefits:
Attribute grammars offer powerful capabilities but also pose challenges:

- Complexity: Writing and managing attribute grammars for complex languages can be challenging due to the intricacies of language rules and the need for attribute propagation strategies.

- Efficiency: Efficient evaluation of attribute grammars is critical for compiler performance, especially in large codebases.

- Clarity and Maintainability: Care must be taken to design attribute grammars that are clear, maintainable, and easy to understand.

Conclusion:
Attribute grammars are the composers of annotations and semantics in the compiler's symphony. They bring life to the static structures of code by attaching meaning and properties. As we journey further into the world of semantic analysis, we will continue to explore the beauty and depth of attribute grammars, uncovering the strategies, techniques, and nuances that enable compilers to master the art of code annotation and interpretation.

VI. Error Checking at the Semantic Level
Unveiling the Deep Layers of Program Understanding Semantic analysis is the phase of the compiler's journey where the program's deeper meaning is unraveled. It's here that the compiler goes beyond the code's mere syntax, diving into its semantics to ensure correctness and reliability. Error checking at the semantic level is an art form that uncovers issues that might remain hidden within the code's syntax, addressing them before they have a chance to manifest during execution.

The Nature of Semantic Errors:
Semantic errors are like hidden traps waiting to ensnare programmers. Unlike syntax errors, which are caught early in the compilation process, semantic errors lurk in the shadows, ready to surface when the code is executed. These errors typically result from incorrect or unexpected behavior based on the code's intended meaning. Common semantic errors include:

1. Type Mismatches: Operations performed on incompatible data types, like trying to add a string to an integer.

2. Undefined Variables: Referencing variables or symbols that have not been declared or are out of scope.

3. Function Signature Mismatches: Calling a function with the wrong number or types of arguments.

4. Memory Management Issues: Failing to allocate or deallocate memory correctly, leading to memory leaks or access violations.

5. Concurrency and Parallelism Errors: Issues related to synchronization, race conditions, and deadlocks in concurrent and parallel programs.

Role of Semantic Error Checking:

1. Detecting Hidden Issues: Semantic error checking uncovers issues that might not be apparent from the code's syntax but can lead to unexpected and incorrect program behavior.

2. Preventing Runtime Crashes: By catching semantic errors at compile-time, it helps prevent runtime crashes and undefined behavior, enhancing the reliability of programs.

3. Improving Code Quality: Identifying and fixing semantic errors leads to cleaner, more robust code and better overall software quality.

Type Checking as a Key Component:
Type checking is a fundamental aspect of semantic error checking. It ensures that operations, expressions, and assignments are performed with compatible data types, in accordance with the language's specifications. Type checking plays a pivotal role in error prevention and detection:

- Type Compatibility: Type checking verifies that the types of operands in expressions match the expected types for the operations being performed.

- Function Signatures: It ensures that functions are called with the correct number and types of arguments and that their return values are used appropriately.

- Variable Declarations: Type checking confirms that variables are declared with a specific type and that they are used consistently with that type.

Static vs. Dynamic Type Checking:

- Static Type Checking: In statically typed languages, type checking occurs at compile-time, ensuring that all type-related issues are caught before the code is executed. This leads to safer and more predictable programs but may require more explicit type annotations.

- Dynamic Type Checking: In dynamically typed languages, type checking occurs at runtime, allowing for more flexibility but potentially leading to runtime errors if type-related issues are not handled gracefully.

Example Scenario:
Consider a snippet in Python:

```python
x = 5
y = "hello"
z = x + y
```

Semantic error checking in Python would catch the type mismatch in the third line when attempting to add an integer and a string.

Challenges and Trade-offs:
Semantic error checking presents challenges and trade-offs:

- Complexity: Handling complex type systems, scoping rules, and language features can be intricate.

- Efficiency: Balancing thorough error checking with compiler performance is essential, especially in large codebases.

- Error Reporting: Providing clear and informative error messages is crucial for programmers to understand and rectify issues.

Conclusion:
Error checking at the semantic level is the compiler's sentinel, guarding against the hidden pitfalls of programming. It goes beyond syntax to explore the code's deeper layers, ensuring that it adheres to its intended meaning and that semantic errors are identified and addressed. As we continue our exploration of semantic analysis, we will delve further into the strategies, techniques, and nuances that compilers employ to master the art of error checking at the semantic level, enhancing the reliability and quality of software.

VII. Intermediate Representations (IR) and Their Role in Optimization
The Compiler's Masterpiece
As we journey deeper into the realm of semantic analysis, we encounter a critical component that transforms the compiler's understanding of code into a

masterpiece of optimization: Intermediate Representations (IR). In this section, we explore the significance of IR and how it serves as the canvas on which compilers create efficient and optimized executables.

The Essence of Intermediate Representations (IR): Intermediate representations are an abstraction layer between the high-level source code and the low-level machine code or assembly language. They provide a structured, language-agnostic representation of the code's semantics, allowing compilers to perform various optimization techniques and code transformations before generating the final executable.

Key Aspects of Intermediate Representations:

1. Language Agnostic: IR is typically designed to be independent of the source programming language. This allows compilers to use a common set of optimization techniques for multiple languages.

2. High-Level Abstraction: IR retains high-level abstractions, such as control flow structures, data structures, and function calls, while avoiding machine-specific details.

3. Optimization Potential: IR is chosen and designed to make optimizations feasible. It often includes information about variable lifetimes, data flow, and control flow, which are crucial for optimization decisions.

4. Intermediate Code Generation: During the compilation process, the source code is translated into IR, which serves as an intermediate step before generating the target machine code.

Role of IR in Optimization:

Intermediate representations play a pivotal role in the optimization phase of compilation. Here's how:

1. Analysis and Transformation: Compilers use IR to perform static analysis of the code, identifying opportunities for optimization. This includes detecting common subexpressions, dead code elimination, and loop optimizations.

2. Target-Independent Optimization: IR enables target-independent optimizations. Optimizations can be applied at this stage without knowledge of the specific machine architecture, making the code more portable.

3. Control Flow and Data Flow Analysis: IR helps compilers analyze control flow and data flow within the program, allowing for optimizations like loop unrolling, constant propagation, and register allocation.

4. High-Level Optimizations: IR preserves high-level abstractions, enabling compilers to perform high-level optimizations such as function inlining, in which small functions are expanded inline for efficiency.

5. Optimization Prerequisites: Some advanced optimizations, such as interprocedural analysis, depend on a common IR to coordinate optimizations across different parts of the codebase.

Types of Intermediate Representations:
Various IR forms exist, each with its own advantages and trade-offs:

1. Abstract Syntax Tree (AST): While not a traditional IR, ASTs are used in some compilers to represent the high-level structure of the code. They are useful for language-agnostic analysis but may lack some details needed for certain optimizations.

2. Three-Address Code (TAC): TAC represents code in a simplified, three-address form, breaking down complex expressions into smaller operations. It's easy to work with and is often used as an intermediate step before more complex IR forms.

3. Static Single Assignment (SSA): SSA form is designed for advanced optimizations. It ensures that each variable is assigned a value only once, simplifying data flow analysis and enabling more aggressive optimizations.

4. Intermediate Language (IL): Some compilers use a high-level intermediate language designed for ease of optimization. Examples include LLVM IR and Java bytecode.

Example of IR in Action:
Consider the following code:

```c
int foo(int x, int y) {
    return x + y;
}
```

In an IR representation, this code might be expressed as:

```
entry:
    param x
    param y
    t1 = x + y
    return t1
```

This representation preserves the essential semantics of the function while abstracting away language-specific details.

Challenges and Benefits:
IR introduces challenges and benefits:

- IR Design: Designing an effective IR is non-trivial, as it must balance expressiveness with optimization potential.

- Compiler Flexibility: A well-designed IR allows compilers to implement a wide range of optimizations, making it a versatile tool for code enhancement.

- Portability: IR enables target-independent optimizations, enhancing code portability.

Conclusion:
Intermediate representations are the canvases on which compilers create their masterpieces of optimization. They serve as a bridge between high-level source code and low-level machine code, preserving semantics while enabling a wealth of code improvements. As we delve deeper into the world of semantic analysis and optimization, we will continue to explore the intricacies of IR, unveiling the strategies, techniques, and nuances that compilers employ to master the art of code enhancement and efficiency.

Chapter 5: Intermediate Code Generation

I. Intermediate Code and Its Purpose
Bridging the Gap Between Source and Machine Code
As we venture further into the compilation process, we encounter a pivotal stage: intermediate code generation. This stage serves as the bridge between the high-level source code and the low-level machine code, enabling compilers to navigate the complexities of optimization, portability, and code generation. In this section, we'll explore the essence of intermediate code and its profound purpose.

The Essence of Intermediate Code:
Intermediate code is an abstract representation of a program that sits between the source code, written by the programmer, and the target code, which is typically machine code or assembly language. It captures the essential semantics of the source code while abstracting away many of the language-specific details.

Key Characteristics of Intermediate Code:

1. Language Agnostic: Intermediate code is designed to be independent of the source programming language, making it suitable for a wide range of languages. This ensures that a single compiler backend can be used for multiple source languages.

2. Human Readable: While not as human-readable as the source code, intermediate code is typically more comprehensible than machine code or assembly language. This aids in debugging and analysis.

3. Optimization-Friendly: Intermediate code is chosen or designed to facilitate various optimization techniques. It retains high-level abstractions and often includes

information about control flow, data flow, and type information.

4. Intermediate Code Generation: During the compilation process, the source code is translated into intermediate code before further transformations and code generation take place.

The Purpose of Intermediate Code:
Intermediate code serves several vital purposes in the compilation process:

1. Abstraction: It abstracts the source code, preserving its essential semantics while discarding many language-specific details. This abstraction simplifies subsequent phases of the compilation process.

2. Portability: Intermediate code enables the compiler to perform target-independent optimizations. These optimizations enhance code portability, as the same intermediate code can be optimized and targeted for different architectures.

3. Optimization: Intermediate code acts as a platform for various optimizations. Compilers can analyze and transform the code at this stage, improving performance, reducing code size, and enhancing code quality.

4. Separation of Concerns: It separates the front end (responsible for parsing, syntax analysis, and semantic analysis) from the back end (responsible for code generation and optimization). This modular design simplifies compiler development and maintenance.

Types of Intermediate Code:
Several forms of intermediate code exist, each with its own characteristics and benefits:

1. Three-Address Code (TAC): TAC is a simple, three-address representation that breaks down complex expressions into smaller operations. It's easy to work with and often used as an initial intermediate form before more complex representations.

2. Static Single Assignment (SSA): SSA form is designed for advanced optimizations. It ensures that each variable is assigned a value only once, simplifying data flow analysis and enabling aggressive optimizations.

3. Intermediate Languages (ILs): Some compilers use high-level intermediate languages designed for ease of optimization. Examples include LLVM IR, Java bytecode, and Microsoft's Common Intermediate Language (CIL).

Example of Intermediate Code:
Consider the following C code:

```c
int main() {
    int x = 5;
    int y = 3;
    int z = x + y;
    return z;
}
```

In an intermediate code representation, this code might look like:

```assembly
_main:
    x = 5
    y = 3
    z = x + y
    return z
```

This intermediate representation captures the essential semantics of the program while abstracting away many of the language-specific details.

Challenges and Trade-offs:
Intermediate code generation presents challenges and trade-offs:

- Design Complexity: Choosing or designing an effective intermediate code representation requires balancing expressiveness with optimization potential.

- Compilation Time: Generating and optimizing intermediate code can increase compilation time, but the benefits often outweigh this drawback.

- Optimization Strategies: The choice of intermediate code representation can influence which optimization strategies can be effectively applied.

Conclusion:
Intermediate code is the conduit through which compilers navigate the complexities of code transformation and optimization. It abstracts the source code's essential semantics, enhances portability, and serves as the foundation for numerous optimization techniques. As we continue our journey into the realm of intermediate code generation, we will explore the intricacies of translating source code into this intermediary form, unveiling the strategies, techniques, and nuances that compilers employ to master the art of code abstraction and optimization.

II. Common Intermediate Representations (e.g., Three-Address Code)
Bridging the Language Gap

In the intricate dance of compilation, the translation of high-level source code into low-level machine code is not an immediate leap. Between these two realms exists a crucial intermediary: the intermediate representation (IR). IRs are the language-agnostic heart of modern compilers, and in this section, we explore one of the most fundamental forms of IR - Three-Address Code (TAC), and its role in the art of intermediate code generation.

The Essence of Three-Address Code (TAC): Three-Address Code (TAC) is a minimalist yet expressive form of intermediate representation that simplifies the complex symphony of high-level programming languages into a three-part harmony. Each TAC statement consists of at most three components, providing a clean and structured way to represent the semantics of source code.

Key Characteristics of TAC:

1. Simplicity: TAC distills complex operations into their essential components, making it easy to understand and manipulate during compilation.

2. Generality: It is designed to be language-agnostic, making it suitable for a wide range of programming languages. This universality allows compiler designers to focus on the commonalities among languages.

3. Ease of Translation: TAC is a natural choice for representing the core logic of source code, which can then be efficiently translated into target-specific assembly code or machine code.

4. Optimization Potential: Despite its simplicity, TAC retains enough high-level semantics to facilitate various

optimization techniques. Its structured nature allows for the efficient application of optimization passes.

Components of TAC:
Each TAC statement consists of three essential components:

1. Operation: This specifies the operation to be performed, such as addition, subtraction, multiplication, or function calls. TAC defines a limited set of operations that can be efficiently translated into target code.

2. Operand 1 and Operand 2: These are the operands or inputs to the operation. They can represent variables, constants, or temporary values generated during compilation. TAC allows for a mix of variables and constants in its operands.

3. Result: The result of the operation is stored in a temporary variable or a memory location. These temporary variables are typically automatically generated by the compiler and have a limited scope and lifetime.

Purpose of TAC:
Three-Address Code serves several vital purposes in the compilation process:

1. Abstraction: TAC abstracts the high-level source code, capturing its essential semantics while shedding much of the language-specific syntax. This abstraction simplifies subsequent phases of the compilation process.

2. Portability: TAC enables the compiler to perform target-independent optimizations. By optimizing the intermediate representation, compilers can generate efficient code for different architectures.

3. Optimization: TAC acts as a platform for various optimization techniques. Compilers can analyze and transform the code at this stage, improving performance, reducing code size, and enhancing code quality.

4. Separation of Concerns: It separates the front end (responsible for parsing, syntax analysis, and semantic analysis) from the back end (responsible for code generation and optimization). This modular design simplifies compiler development and maintenance.

Example of TAC in Action:
Consider a simple C code snippet:

```c
int x = 5;
int y = 3;
int z = x + y;
```

In Three-Address Code, this code might look like:

```
t1 = 5
t2 = 3
t3 = t1 + t2
```

Each TAC statement represents a step in the computation, abstracting away language-specific details.

Challenges and Trade-offs:
While Three-Address Code provides significant benefits, it also presents challenges:

- Limited Expressiveness: TAC may not fully capture the high-level semantics of some complex languages, requiring additional IR forms or extensions for certain optimizations.

- Code Size: TAC can introduce temporary variables, potentially increasing code size. However, this can be mitigated through later optimization phases.

- Debugging: Debugging at the TAC level can be more challenging than debugging at the source code level due to the abstraction of language-specific constructs.

Conclusion:
Three-Address Code stands as a bridge between the diverse symphonies of high-level programming languages and the precision of machine code. Its simplicity, generality, and optimization potential make it a powerful choice for representing the essential semantics of source code. As we continue our exploration of intermediate code generation, we will uncover the intricacies of translating source code into TAC, unveiling the strategies, techniques, and nuances that compilers employ to master the art of abstraction and optimization.

III. Translation of High-Level Code into Intermediate Code
The Art of Abstraction

At the heart of the compiler's transformational journey lies the intricate process of translating high-level source code into an intermediate representation (IR). This phase, often referred to as "Intermediate Code Generation," is a pivotal step that bridges the gap between the human-readable abstractions of programming languages and the machine-understandable intricacies of assembly or machine code. In this section, we embark on a journey into the art and science of translating high-level code into intermediate code.

The Essence of Intermediate Code:
Intermediate code serves as an abstraction layer that encapsulates the essential semantics of the high-level source code while stripping away much of the language-specific syntax. It provides a structured and uniform representation of the code's logic, making it amenable to subsequent optimization and code generation steps.

Key Considerations in Translation:
The translation of high-level code into intermediate code is a complex task, influenced by various considerations:

1. Syntax Analysis: The compiler's front end, responsible for parsing and syntax analysis, ensures that the source code adheres to the language's grammar and generates a parse tree or an abstract syntax tree (AST).

2. Semantic Analysis: After parsing, the compiler performs semantic analysis to ensure that the code adheres to language-specific rules, such as type checking, variable scoping, and error checking.

3. Intermediate Representation (IR) Selection: The choice of an appropriate IR form, such as Three-Address Code (TAC), Static Single Assignment (SSA), or an intermediate language (IL), is crucial. The selection depends on factors like optimization goals and the target architecture.

4. Expression Translation: Expressions in the source code are translated into a series of intermediate code instructions, preserving their semantics. For example, addition, subtraction, and multiplication operations are mapped to the corresponding IR operations.

5. Control Flow Translation: Control structures, including conditionals (if-else statements) and loops, are

translated into intermediate code that manages program flow and logic.

6. Error Handling: During translation, the compiler must detect and handle errors, such as syntax errors, type mismatches, and undeclared identifiers. Clear and informative error messages are generated to aid programmers in debugging.

Example of Translation:
Consider a simple C code snippet:

```c
int add(int a, int b) {
    return a + b;
}
```

The translation process might produce intermediate code like this (using a simplified representation):

```
Function add
Parameters: a, b
Begin:
    t1 = a + b
    Return t1
End
```

Here, we've abstracted away the C-specific syntax and retained the essence of the function: it takes two integers as input, performs addition, and returns the result.

Benefits of Intermediate Code:

1. Abstraction: Intermediate code abstracts the essential program logic, making it easier to reason about, manipulate, and optimize.

2. Portability: By translating high-level code into an intermediate form, compilers can perform target-independent optimizations, enhancing code portability.

3. Optimization: Intermediate code serves as a platform for various optimization techniques. Optimizations applied at this stage can have a significant impact on the final code's performance.

4. Separation of Concerns: The translation process separates the front end (parsing, syntax analysis, and semantic analysis) from the back end (code generation and optimization), facilitating modular compiler design.

Challenges and Trade-offs:
Translating high-level code into intermediate code presents challenges:

- Expressiveness: Ensuring that the intermediate code fully captures the high-level semantics of the source language can be challenging, especially for complex languages.

- Efficiency: Generating efficient intermediate code that minimizes redundant operations and temporary variables is essential for optimization.

- Debugging: Debugging at the intermediate code level may be more challenging than at the source code level due to the abstraction of language-specific constructs.

Conclusion:
The translation of high-level code into intermediate code is the initial step in the transformational journey of a

compiler. It involves abstracting the code's essential semantics, enabling portability, optimization, and separation of concerns. As we delve deeper into the world of intermediate code generation, we will explore the intricacies of translating diverse programming languages into structured, language-agnostic representations, unveiling the strategies, techniques, and nuances that compilers employ to master the art of abstraction and optimization.

IV. Handling Expressions, Control Flow, and Procedures in Intermediate Code

The Compiler's Choreography

In the grand ballet of compilation, where high-level source code transforms into intricate machine instructions, the handling of expressions, control flow, and procedures is a choreographic masterpiece. This delicate process involves translating the rich tapestry of programming constructs into an intermediate code representation. In this section, we explore the art and intricacies of managing expressions, control flow, and procedures in intermediate code.

Expressions in Intermediate Code:
Expressions are the melodies that compose the language of computation, and they form an integral part of any program. In the realm of intermediate code, expressions need to be abstracted and transformed into a structured format that retains their essential semantics while being amenable to subsequent optimization and code generation.

1. Translating Arithmetic Expressions: Arithmetic expressions, such as addition, subtraction, multiplication, and division, must be translated into sequences of intermediate code instructions. For example, the expression `x + y` in the source code might translate into

`t1 = x + y` in the intermediate code, where `t1` represents a temporary variable.

2. Handling Function Calls: Function calls, both for user-defined functions and library functions, necessitate the generation of intermediate code to manage parameter passing, return values, and control flow. This typically involves creating a function call instruction, pushing parameters onto a stack or registers, and handling the return value.

Control Flow in Intermediate Code:
Control flow orchestrates the program's journey, directing its execution along the paths defined by conditionals, loops, and branches. The translation of control flow constructs is a delicate dance in the realm of intermediate code.

1. Conditional Statements: If-else statements and switch cases in the source code must be translated into conditional branches in intermediate code. For instance, the source code `if (x > 0) { /* code */ }` translates into a conditional branch in intermediate code, where the branch target depends on the evaluation of `x > 0`.

2. Loops: While loops, for loops, and other loop constructs are translated into intermediate code that manages the loop condition and loop body. Loop variables, initialization, and iteration logic are abstracted and represented in the intermediate code.

3. Branching and Jumping: Control flow statements like `goto` in some languages are translated into branch or jump instructions in intermediate code, directing the program's flow to the specified label or target.

Procedures and Functions in Intermediate Code:

Procedures and functions compose the chapters of modularity in programming, encapsulating logic into reusable units. Handling procedures in intermediate code involves creating an abstraction that supports parameter passing, local variable management, and function calls.

1. Function Declarations: When a function is declared, its signature, return type, and parameter list must be translated into intermediate code to aid in function call resolution and type checking.

2. Function Calls: Invoking a function entails generating intermediate code for parameter passing, managing the function's activation record (stack frame), and handling return values.

3. Local Variables: Local variables within functions require memory allocation in the function's stack frame and translations of assignments and references into intermediate code instructions.

Optimization and Intermediate Code:
Intermediate code acts as a platform for optimization, allowing compilers to apply various transformations to enhance program performance. Expressions, control flow, and procedures within the intermediate representation can be optimized for efficiency and code quality.

1. Expression Simplification: Redundant expressions or subexpressions can be eliminated, and constants can be folded to optimize arithmetic operations.

2. Control Flow Analysis: Control flow constructs can be analyzed to identify opportunities for loop unrolling, dead code elimination, and branch optimization.

3. Procedure Inlining: In some cases, small functions can be inlined, reducing the overhead of function calls.

Challenges and Trade-offs:
Handling expressions, control flow, and procedures in intermediate code generation presents challenges:

- Complexity: Accurately representing the intricacies of high-level constructs while abstracting away language-specific details is a complex task.

- Optimization vs. Readability: Balancing the optimization potential of intermediate code with its readability for debugging and analysis is a challenge.

- Target Independence: Ensuring that intermediate code is sufficiently target-independent for optimization can be demanding.

Conclusion:
The handling of expressions, control flow, and procedures in intermediate code is a dance of abstraction and transformation. It requires translating the nuanced language of high-level programming into a structured, language-agnostic representation. As we continue our exploration of intermediate code generation, we will delve deeper into the intricacies of managing these critical aspects, unveiling the strategies, techniques, and nuances that compilers employ to master the art of orchestration in the realm of intermediate code.

V. Generating Code for Various Programming Language Constructs
The Multilingual Choreography
In the intricate world of compiler design, the generation of intermediate code stands as the first act in the grand performance of code transformation. Yet, the true artistry

of a compiler unfolds in the generation of code for various programming language constructs. This chapter explores the nuances of this choreography—translating the rich diversity of high-level language constructs into an intermediate form that transcends language barriers.

The Polyglot Compiler's Dilemma:
One of the remarkable feats of a compiler is its ability to handle an array of programming languages. The source code it encounters can range from the structured syntax of C to the dynamic expressiveness of Python, the object-oriented elegance of Java, or the functional purity of Haskell. Each language comes with its unique features and syntactic quirks, making the compiler's task of code generation akin to orchestrating a multilingual ballet.

Handling Expressions:
Expressions form the foundation of programming, and their translation into intermediate code involves an intricate choreography:

1. Arithmetic Expressions: The compiler must understand how to translate arithmetic operations (+, -, *, /) from each language into a series of intermediate code instructions. For instance, the expression `a + b` in C might translate into `t1 = a + b` in intermediate code.

2. Logical Expressions: Logic expressions (e.g., `&&`, `||`, `!`) in languages like C, Java, or Python need to be appropriately translated into intermediate code, preserving their semantic meaning.

3. Function Calls: Different languages employ various function call conventions, and the compiler must generate intermediate code that adheres to these conventions. This includes parameter passing, return value handling, and stack management.

Control Flow Choreography:
Control flow structures—such as conditionals and loops —require meticulous choreography to ensure the program's logic is accurately captured:

1. Conditionals: Languages offer a range of conditional constructs, from C's `if-else` to Python's `if-elif-else`. The compiler must map these to conditional branches in the intermediate code, appropriately branching to the target labels.

2. Loop Constructs: The compiler must understand how each language defines and iterates over loops (e.g., `for`, `while`, `do-while`) and translate them into intermediate code that handles loop conditions and iterations.

3. Switch Statements: Languages like C and C++ feature switch statements, which require special handling to map case labels and fallthrough logic into intermediate code.

Procedures and Functions:
The generation of code for procedures and functions involves a careful ballet of managing local variables, parameter passing, and function calls:

1. Parameter Passing: Languages may use different conventions for parameter passing, including pass by value, pass by reference, or pass by name. The compiler must generate intermediate code that respects these conventions.

2. Local Variable Management: The allocation and management of local variables within functions or methods must be accurately represented in the intermediate code.

3. Function Overloading and Polymorphism: Some languages support function overloading or polymorphism, where the same function name may have different implementations. The compiler must generate code that respects these language-specific rules.

Optimizing the Multilingual Ballet:
Optimization is a universal pursuit in compiler design. The compiler's choreography of generating intermediate code for various programming language constructs plays a pivotal role in enabling optimization:

1. Expression Simplification: The compiler can simplify expressions by eliminating redundancy, performing constant folding, and optimizing arithmetic operations.

2. Control Flow Optimization: Control flow structures, when translated into intermediate code, can be optimized to reduce branch instructions, eliminate unreachable code, and enhance loop structures.

3. Inlining and Function Optimization: In some cases, functions may be inlined to eliminate the overhead of function calls, and function bodies may be optimized for efficiency.

Conclusion:
Generating code for various programming language constructs is the compiler's multilingual choreography, where diverse languages come together to create a symphony of instructions in the universal language of intermediate code. It requires a deep understanding of each language's features, conventions, and idiosyncrasies. As we venture further into the world of intermediate code generation, we will explore the techniques, strategies, and nuances that enable compilers to master the art of code generation, ensuring

that the richness and diversity of programming languages are elegantly captured in the final performance of the compiled program.

Chapter 6: Code Optimization

I. Importance of Code Optimization
Crafting Efficient Masterpieces
In the intricate symphony of compiler design, the code optimization phase emerges as a virtuoso performance. It is here that the raw potential of a program is refined into an efficient masterpiece. Code optimization, often considered the heart of a compiler, is the process of enhancing a program's performance, reducing its memory footprint, and improving its execution speed. This chapter delves deep into the profound significance of code optimization in the world of software engineering.

The Compiler's Crucial Role:
Code optimization is a transformative stage in the compilation process, and its importance cannot be overstated. Compilers serve as the conductors of this symphony, orchestrating a harmonious blend of techniques and algorithms to refine the code's performance. Here's why code optimization is pivotal:

1. Efficiency and Speed: Optimized code runs faster. It can make the difference between a program that responds promptly and one that lags behind, frustrating users. In real-time systems, such as embedded software or video games, speed is of the essence. Code optimization can make these systems responsive and efficient.

2. Resource Conservation: Optimization reduces a program's memory footprint, which is crucial in resource-constrained environments. Smaller memory requirements mean more resources available for other tasks or for accommodating larger datasets.

3. Energy Efficiency: In the era of mobile devices and cloud computing, energy efficiency is paramount. Optimized code consumes less power, extending battery life on mobile devices and reducing electricity costs in data centers.

4. Cost Savings: Faster and more efficient code requires fewer computational resources. This translates into cost savings in terms of hardware, infrastructure, and energy consumption.

5. Competitive Edge: In the highly competitive software market, performance is often a key differentiator. Users expect responsive and efficient applications. Code optimization can give a product a competitive edge.

6. Scalability: As programs grow in complexity, optimization becomes essential for maintaining acceptable performance levels. Without optimization, software may become sluggish and impractical to use.

Optimization Techniques:
The art and science of code optimization encompass a rich array of techniques and strategies. Some of the most common include:

1. Constant Folding: Evaluating and simplifying constant expressions during compilation, reducing runtime computation.

2. Common Subexpression Elimination: Identifying and eliminating redundant calculations to reduce computational overhead.

3. Dead Code Elimination: Removing code that cannot be executed, reducing program size and enhancing clarity.

4. Loop Optimization: Transforming loops to minimize overhead, enhance cache locality, and reduce loop-invariant computations.

5. Register Allocation: Efficiently managing the limited number of registers available on a CPU to minimize memory accesses and improve performance.

6. Inline Function Expansion: Replacing function calls with the actual function code to eliminate call overhead, a technique often used for small, frequently called functions.

7. Data Flow Analysis: Analyzing how data flows through a program to identify optimization opportunities and uncover dependencies.

8. Code Reordering: Reorganizing code to optimize instruction scheduling and reduce pipeline stalls in modern processors.

9. High-Level Language Optimization: Leveraging language-specific optimizations that exploit high-level language features for performance improvements.

10. Profile-Guided Optimization (PGO): Using profiling information gathered during program execution to guide optimizations, adapting the code for specific usage patterns.

Conclusion:
Code optimization is the virtuoso performance of the compiler, where raw code is transformed into an efficient masterpiece. Its importance extends beyond mere performance gains; it impacts resource utilization, energy efficiency, cost savings, and competitiveness. In the fast-paced world of software development, optimization is the key to crafting software that not only

functions but excels. As we journey deeper into the realm of code optimization, we will explore the techniques, principles, and intricacies that enable compilers to orchestrate this symphony of efficiency, ensuring that every line of code is fine-tuned to perfection.

II. Common Optimization Techniques
Refining the Art of Efficiency
In the realm of compiler design, the optimization phase is where the magic happens. It's the place where the rough drafts of code are transformed into efficient masterpieces. This chapter explores some of the most common optimization techniques, the brushstrokes and strokes of genius that enhance a program's performance, reduce its resource consumption, and bring out the elegance hidden within its lines of code.

Constant Folding: The Art of Precomputation
Constant Folding is a technique that allows the compiler to perform calculations at compile-time instead of runtime. This optimization is particularly effective when dealing with expressions involving constants. Here's how it works:

Imagine a simple expression like `3 * 4`. In a naive interpretation, this would be evaluated at runtime, but constant folding steps in, recognizing that both operands are constants. It replaces the expression with its computed value, `12`, at compile-time.

Now, consider a more complex expression: `2 * (3 + 4)`. Constant folding will break this down, calculating `3 + 4` to `7` and replacing the expression with `2 * 7`, which equals `14`. The result is a simpler and more efficient representation of the computation.

Common Subexpression Elimination: The Art of Recognizing Redundancy

In many programs, especially those with loops or repeated calculations, it's common to encounter redundant subexpressions. Common Subexpression Elimination (CSE) is the technique that seeks out these redundancies and eliminates them.

Imagine a loop that calculates `x * y` multiple times within its body. CSE recognizes that the same subexpression is being recomputed and introduces a temporary variable to store the result of `x * y`. Now, instead of recalculating it each time, the loop references the temporary variable, significantly reducing computational overhead.

Dead Code Elimination: The Art of Cleaning House

Dead code is the unused, unnecessary portion of a program that can clutter the codebase and waste precious computational resources. Dead Code Elimination identifies and removes such code, reducing program size and improving code clarity.

Consider a program that contains conditional blocks with unreachable code. Dead Code Elimination detects this unreachable code and prunes it, reducing the program's memory footprint and enhancing its maintainability.

Loop Optimization: The Art of Efficiency in Iteration

Loops are the workhorses of many programs, and optimizing them can yield substantial performance improvements. Loop Optimization involves a range of techniques:

- Loop Unrolling: This technique involves expanding a loop by a factor of `n`, reducing loop control overhead and improving cache locality. For instance, a loop that iterates ten times might be unrolled to execute five times, each time processing two iterations.

- Loop Fusion and Fission: Loop Fusion combines multiple loops into a single loop to reduce loop overhead, while Loop Fission splits a single loop into multiple loops to improve data locality and parallelism.

- Loop-Invariant Code Motion (LICM): LICM identifies and moves loop-invariant code (code that produces the same result in each iteration) outside of the loop. This reduces redundant computations and enhances performance.

Register Allocation: The Art of Efficient Use of Resources
Registers are precious resources in computer architecture, and efficient Register Allocation is crucial for optimization. This technique assigns variables and temporary values to registers to minimize memory access and enhance execution speed.

Imagine a program with numerous variables and intermediate values. Register Allocation optimally maps these to the limited number of available registers, reducing memory traffic and optimizing the program's performance.

Conclusion: The Symphony of Optimization
These common optimization techniques represent the harmonious composition of compiler design, where redundancy is eliminated, computations are streamlined, and resources are utilized efficiently. Through Constant Folding, Common Subexpression Elimination, Dead Code Elimination, Loop Optimization, and Register Allocation, compilers conduct a symphony of efficiency that transforms raw code into eloquent, high-performance software.

As we delve deeper into the world of code optimization, we will explore advanced techniques and strategies that further refine this symphony, ensuring that every line of code is finely tuned to perfection.

III. Control Flow Analysis and Optimization

Directing the Flow of Efficiency

In the symphony of code optimization, control flow analysis and optimization are the conductors that direct the flow of efficiency throughout a program. This chapter explores the intricacies of understanding and enhancing the program's control flow, a pivotal aspect of optimization that can significantly impact a program's performance and resource utilization.

Understanding Control Flow: The Program's Rhythm

Control flow in a program dictates the order in which instructions are executed. It encompasses the conditional branches, loops, function calls, and jumps that orchestrate a program's execution. Optimizing control flow involves orchestrating this symphony for efficiency.

Control Flow Analysis: Unveiling Program Behavior

Control flow analysis is the process of understanding and characterizing a program's control flow. This analysis provides critical insights into the program's behavior, enabling subsequent optimizations. Here are some essential aspects of control flow analysis:

1. Control Flow Graph (CFG): A Control Flow Graph is a graphical representation of a program's control flow. It consists of nodes (basic blocks) connected by edges (control flow transitions). CFGs provide a visual overview of how the program's control flows from one instruction to another.

2. Dominators and Post-dominators: Dominators are blocks that control the flow to all other blocks in a CFG. Post-dominators are blocks that control the flow out of all other blocks. These concepts are crucial for various optimization techniques.

3. Loops and Loop Analysis: Identifying loops and analyzing their behavior is fundamental for loop optimization. Techniques like loop unrolling and loop fusion rely on loop analysis.

4. Data-flow Analysis: Data-flow analysis examines how data propagates through a program. It helps identify opportunities for optimizations like constant propagation and dead code elimination.

Control Flow Optimization: The Conductor's Baton Control flow optimization is the art of improving a program's efficiency by manipulating its control flow. This optimization focuses on enhancing the program's execution speed, reducing branch mispredictions, and minimizing unnecessary jumps. Here are some key control flow optimization techniques:

1. Conditional Branch Optimization: Conditional branches are a critical part of control flow. Techniques like branch prediction and branch target prediction aim to reduce the performance impact of conditional branches.

2. Loop Optimization: Loops are often the performance bottlenecks in programs. Loop optimization techniques, such as loop unrolling, loop fusion, and loop-invariant code motion, seek to make loops more efficient.

3. Control-Flow Simplification: Simplifying control flow structures can reduce execution overhead. Techniques like if-conversion and conditional move instructions aim to eliminate unnecessary branches and jumps.

4. Procedure Inlining: Inlining involves replacing a function call with the function's code. This optimization reduces the overhead of function calls, especially for small, frequently called functions.

5. Control-Flow Graph Transformations: Transforming the control flow graph can optimize control flow. Techniques like tail call optimization, function cloning, and function reordering can improve control flow efficiency.

6. Profile-Guided Optimization (PGO): PGO uses runtime profiling information to guide control flow optimizations. It adapts the program's control flow based on its actual usage patterns.

Conclusion: The Maestro's Touch
Control flow analysis and optimization are the maestro's touch in the symphony of code optimization. These techniques, rooted in deep understanding and meticulous orchestration of a program's control flow, can lead to substantial performance gains. As we journey further into the world of code optimization, we will explore advanced techniques and strategies that allow compilers to finely tune the control flow, ensuring that programs execute with precision and efficiency, like a well-conducted orchestra.

III. Data Flow Analysis and Optimization
The Symphony of Efficiency
In the grand composition of code optimization, data flow analysis and optimization play the role of harmonious instruments, guiding the flow of data through a program. This chapter explores the intricate world of data flow analysis—a crucial aspect of optimizing code for efficiency and resource utilization.

Understanding Data Flow: The Pulse of a Program
Data flow is the lifeblood of a program, representing how data values propagate through its instructions. Understanding data flow is essential for identifying optimization opportunities, enhancing performance, and minimizing resource consumption.

IV. Data Flow Analysis

The Art of Insight
Data flow analysis is a systematic examination of how data values evolve as a program executes. It provides valuable insights into variables' lifetimes, dependencies, and potential optimization points. Key concepts in data flow analysis include:

1. Reaching Definitions: Reaching definitions analysis identifies the points in a program where a variable is defined before it is used. This information helps optimize variable usage, enabling the elimination of redundant assignments.

2. Live Variables: Live variables analysis identifies points in the program where a variable's value remains relevant. This knowledge is critical for optimizing memory usage and variable lifetimes.

3. Available Expressions: Available expressions analysis identifies expressions that can be computed at a particular program point without re-evaluation. This optimization eliminates redundant calculations.

4. Data Flow Graphs: Data flow analysis often uses data flow graphs or equations to represent how data values propagate through the program. These graphs illustrate the relationships between program elements, aiding in optimization decisions.

Data Flow Optimization: The Symphony's Crescendo

Data flow optimization is the process of improving a program's efficiency by optimizing the flow and usage of data values. These optimizations focus on minimizing redundant computations, optimizing memory usage, and improving overall program performance. Here are some key data flow optimization techniques:

1. Constant Propagation: Constant propagation optimizes by replacing variables with their constant values when known. This reduces the number of memory accesses and redundant computations.

2. Copy Propagation: Copy propagation replaces variables with the values they hold when possible. This optimization reduces memory usage and eliminates unnecessary data copying.

3. Dead Code Elimination: Dead code elimination identifies and removes code that cannot be reached or executed, enhancing program clarity and resource efficiency.

4. Redundant Code Elimination: Redundant code elimination targets expressions that are computed more than once without changes. By eliminating redundancy, this optimization reduces computational overhead.

5. Memory Optimization: Data flow analysis can be used to optimize memory allocation and deallocation by identifying when memory is no longer needed and releasing it.

6. Induction Variable Elimination: This optimization targets loop induction variables and eliminates unnecessary calculations, reducing loop overhead.

7. Sparse Conditional Constant Propagation (SCCP): SCCP is an advanced technique that combines constant

propagation and control flow analysis to determine the most precise constant values at each program point.

Conclusion: The Symphony's Resolution
Data flow analysis and optimization are the crescendo in the symphony of code optimization. These techniques, grounded in the understanding of data propagation, fine-tune a program's efficiency and resource utilization. They transform a cacophony of data values into a harmonious melody of optimized code. As we delve further into the world of code optimization, we will explore advanced techniques and strategies that harness the power of data flow analysis to create programs that execute with precision and efficiency, like a beautifully orchestrated symphony.

V. Loop Optimization
The Rhapsody of Efficiency
Within the realm of code optimization, loops represent the recurring motifs in a program's composition. Loop optimization, often regarded as one of the most intricate and impactful facets of code enhancement, is akin to composing a rhapsody of efficiency. This chapter uncovers the art and science of loop optimization—an endeavor that can significantly elevate a program's performance.

The Pervasive Role of Loops: A Musical Leitmotif
Loops are the backbone of many programs, enabling repetitive execution of code. They encapsulate the essence of iteration and are the workhorses that drive computations, data processing, and algorithmic implementations. However, their ubiquity also makes them prime candidates for optimization.

Understanding Loop Optimization: The Composer's Perspective

Loop optimization is a composer's endeavor, aimed at harmonizing loops with the orchestra of computational resources. This optimization symphony focuses on streamlining loop structures, minimizing overhead, enhancing cache locality, and reducing computational burdens.

Key Loop Optimization Techniques: Composing the Sonata

1. Loop Unrolling: Loop unrolling is like extending a musical phrase, allowing it to play more notes with fewer pauses. In this optimization, the loop body is replicated multiple times within the loop, reducing loop control overhead and improving instruction scheduling. For instance, a loop that iterates ten times might be unrolled to execute five times, each time processing two iterations.

2. Loop Fusion: Loop fusion combines multiple loops into a single loop. It's akin to blending musical themes to create a harmonious melody. By reducing loop overhead and enhancing data locality, loop fusion optimizes memory access patterns and can improve cache utilization.

3. Loop Fission: Loop fission is the opposite of fusion, breaking a single loop into multiple loops. This optimization can improve data locality and parallelism by dividing a complex loop into smaller, more manageable parts.

4. Loop-Invariant Code Motion (LICM): LICM identifies code within a loop that produces the same result in every iteration and moves it outside the loop. This optimization eliminates redundant computations and can significantly reduce the overall computational burden.

5. Array and Data Structure Transformation: This technique involves transforming data structures or arrays to improve data locality. It can enhance cache performance and reduce memory latency.

6. Loop Tiling: Loop tiling divides a loop into smaller tiles, optimizing memory access patterns and improving cache usage. This optimization is particularly useful for nested loops.

7. Parallelization: Loop optimization can also involve parallelizing loops to leverage multiple processing cores or units, enhancing computational throughput.

Loop-Carried Dependencies: The Harmonic Constraints
In the world of loop optimization, loop-carried dependencies are the dissonant notes that can challenge the composer. These dependencies represent data or control flow dependencies that span multiple iterations of a loop, limiting the extent to which a loop can be optimized.

Conclusion: The Symphony's Crescendo
Loop optimization is the crescendo in the symphony of code optimization. It is a composition of meticulous techniques, aiming to transform repetitive iterations into an orchestrated masterpiece of efficiency. As we delve deeper into the world of code optimization, we will explore advanced loop optimization strategies and techniques that allow compilers to fine-tune loops to perfection, ensuring that they play their part in the symphony of high-performance software.

VI. Measuring and Evaluating the Effectiveness of Optimizations
In the intricate domain of code optimization within compilers, the pursuit of efficiency and performance hinges upon the ability to systematically measure and

evaluate the efficacy of optimizations. This critical process forms the crucible in which the alchemical transformation of raw code into highly efficient and streamlined executable programs occurs. Let us delve into the nuanced world of measuring and evaluating the effectiveness of optimizations in the context of compiler code optimization.

Quantifying the Impact:
At the core of measuring optimization effectiveness lies the need to quantify the impact of each transformation. This begins with establishing baseline metrics, encompassing factors such as execution time, memory utilization, and computational resources. These metrics serve as reference points against which the effects of optimizations are benchmarked.

Benchmarking as a Pillar:
Benchmarking emerges as an indispensable pillar in the evaluation of optimization outcomes. It involves the selection of representative input programs that simulate real-world usage scenarios. These benchmarks serve as the litmus test for optimization, reflecting how well the compiler's output performs under various conditions. The systematic application of optimizations to these benchmarks enables a comparative analysis that reveals the true extent of improvement.

Profiling Insights:
Profiling tools play a pivotal role in the assessment of optimization effectiveness. Profilers gather data on program behavior, revealing performance bottlenecks, resource usage patterns, and execution paths. This data forms the foundation for evaluating the impact of optimizations, allowing developers to pinpoint areas of code that benefit the most from optimization efforts.

Before-and-After Comparison:

The narrative of optimization unfolds through the before-and-after comparison of code. This involves measuring the performance and resource utilization of the original, unoptimized code and contrasting it with the optimized version. Metrics such as execution time reduction, memory footprint reduction, and CPU utilization changes provide a tangible gauge of optimization success.

Strategies for Rigorous Evaluation:
Systematic performance testing strategies are crucial for comprehensive evaluation. A/B testing methodologies are employed to rigorously compare the optimized and unoptimized versions of a program under diverse workloads and input datasets. This approach ensures that optimizations are robust and consistently yield benefits across various scenarios.

Empirical Analysis:
The empirical analysis of optimization effectiveness involves studying real-world case studies. These empirical insights often shape the direction of compiler optimizations. Examining how optimizations have influenced the performance of renowned compilers provides valuable lessons and benchmarks for future efforts.

Addressing Limitations and Trade-offs:
Optimization is not a one-size-fits-all endeavor, and understanding its limitations and trade-offs is imperative. Some optimizations may not yield significant benefits in certain contexts or may introduce unexpected side effects. Thorough evaluation helps identify scenarios where optimization may not be advantageous.

The Role of Reporting:
Optimization evaluation culminates in meticulous reporting. Standardized formats and metrics facilitate clear and consistent communication of results. Proper

reporting ensures that optimization strategies are transparent, reproducible, and subject to peer scrutiny.

Conclusion:
In the complex realm of compiler code optimization, measuring and evaluating the effectiveness of optimizations is both a science and an art. It is a process that demands a keen understanding of program behavior, meticulous benchmarking, and a discerning eye for trade-offs and limitations. By employing these methodologies, compilers strive to transmute code into its most efficient form, thereby contributing to the ever-evolving landscape of software efficiency and performance.

Chapter 7: Code Generation

I. Code Generation Phase

Forging the Heart of Executables

In the symphony of compiler construction, the code generation phase takes center stage, serving as the artisanal craftsperson who forges the heart of executable programs. This chapter delves into the vital role of the code generation phase, where high-level abstractions are transformed into machine-executable instructions, breathing life into software.

The Essence of Code Generation: From High-Level to Low-Level

The code generation phase bridges the gap between high-level programming languages and the intricate world of machine code. Its primary objective is to produce machine-executable instructions that faithfully represent the functionality and behavior of the source program.

Code Generation Tasks: Crafting the Blueprint of Execution

1. Instruction Selection: At the core of code generation lies the task of selecting appropriate machine instructions to represent high-level language constructs. This process involves mapping high-level operations, such as addition or conditional branching, to the corresponding machine instructions of the target architecture.

2. Register Allocation: Modern processors typically have a limited number of registers, and efficient register allocation is crucial. This task assigns variables and temporary values to registers, minimizing memory access and optimizing execution speed.

3. Addressing Modes: Memory access is a critical aspect of code generation. Addressing modes determine how variables and data are accessed in memory, including direct addressing, indirect addressing, and indexed addressing.

4. Code Optimization: Code generation often includes optimization techniques aimed at producing efficient machine code. These techniques may involve instruction scheduling, peephole optimization, and target-specific optimizations.

Target Architecture Considerations: The Blueprint for Execution

The target architecture significantly influences the code generation process. Different processors have distinct instruction sets, addressing modes, and architectural features that demand specific code generation strategies. A compiler must be aware of these nuances to generate efficient code for the target platform.

Code Generation Challenges: The Complexity of Translation

1. Expression Evaluation: Translating complex expressions involving multiple operators and operands into a sequence of machine instructions requires careful consideration of operator precedence, associativity, and temporary value storage.

2. Control Flow: Code generation for control flow structures, such as conditionals and loops, necessitates the generation of appropriate branching and jump instructions to direct program flow accurately.

3. Data Management: Handling data of various types, including integers, floating-point numbers, and complex

data structures, involves generating code for memory allocation, data copying, and data manipulation.

4. Function Calls: Generating code for function calls involves pushing arguments onto the stack, managing the call stack, and ensuring proper return address handling.

The Role of Code Generation in Producing Executable Code

The code generation phase is the culmination of the compiler's efforts. It transforms the abstract representation of a program into a tangible, machine-executable form. The generated code is the embodiment of the software's logic, behavior, and functionality, ready to be executed by the target machine.

The resulting executable code carries the responsibility of faithfully executing the original program's intent. It must adhere to the semantics of the source language, handle data efficiently, and navigate control flow accurately. Additionally, the code generator strives to produce code that is not only correct but also optimized for performance.

Conclusion: The Art of Code Forging

The code generation phase stands as the artisan's workshop in the compiler's journey, where high-level abstractions are meticulously translated into machine-executable instructions. It is the phase where the blueprint of execution is crafted, transforming software from abstract concepts into tangible, functional programs. As we venture further into the world of code generation, we will explore advanced techniques, optimizations, and target-specific considerations that empower compilers to master this artistry, ensuring the creation of efficient and performant executables.

II. Target Machine Architecture and Instruction Set

The Canvas of Execution

In the intricate symphony of compiler construction, understanding the target machine architecture and instruction set architecture is akin to knowing the canvas, brushes, and colors for a masterpiece. This chapter unveils the pivotal role of comprehending the intricacies of the target machine architecture in the code generation phase, where the artistry of crafting executable code unfolds.

The Target Machine: Where Code Finds Its Home

A compiler's primary objective is to translate high-level source code into machine-executable instructions. To achieve this, it must intimately understand the target machine—the hardware on which the generated code will run. Here are the key components that constitute the target machine:

1. Instruction Set Architecture (ISA): The ISA is the foundation of a processor's programming model. It defines the set of instructions, their formats, and their behavior. Each processor family has its own unique ISA, which dictates the operations that can be performed and how they are encoded.

2. Memory Hierarchy: The memory hierarchy, including the processor's cache levels, main memory, and secondary storage, influences data access patterns and memory management. An efficient code generator must consider these aspects to minimize memory latency and optimize data access.

3. Registers: Registers are small, fast storage locations within the CPU. They play a critical role in instruction execution and data manipulation. The number of registers, their usage conventions, and their capabilities vary among processor architectures.

4. Addressing Modes: Addressing modes define how memory addresses are computed for data access. They determine how operands are fetched and stored, which can significantly impact code generation.

Instruction Set Architecture (ISA): The Language of the Machine

The ISA is the language spoken by the target machine, comprising a set of instructions that the processor can execute. Understanding the ISA is paramount for a code generator, as it dictates how high-level language constructs are translated into machine code. Key aspects of ISA include:

1. Instruction Types: ISAs encompass various instruction types, including data transfer, arithmetic and logic operations, control flow, and system instructions. A code generator must select the appropriate instructions to implement high-level language constructs.

2. Operand Types: ISAs define the types of operands an instruction can operate on, such as integers, floating-point numbers, or memory addresses. The code generator must ensure compatibility between operands and instructions.

3. Addressing Modes: Addressing modes specify how memory operands are addressed. These modes can be immediate (constants), direct (explicit memory addresses), or indexed (address computations). The code generator must generate code that adheres to the target machine's addressing modes.

4. Control Flow Instructions: ISAs include instructions for branching, conditional execution, and function calls. The code generator must emit code that correctly implements the program's control flow logic.

Register Allocation: The Maestro's Baton
The number and capabilities of registers available in the
target machine greatly influence code generation.
Efficient register allocation is essential to minimize
memory access and optimize execution speed. Register
allocation strategies must take into account the target
machine's register file size, usage conventions, and
support for operations like SIMD (Single Instruction,
Multiple Data).

Target-Specific Optimizations: The Art of Tailoring
Understanding the intricacies of the target machine
allows for the implementation of target-specific
optimizations. These optimizations leverage the unique
features and capabilities of the hardware to enhance
code performance. Examples include vectorization for
SIMD architectures and instruction scheduling to exploit
pipeline parallelism.

Conclusion: The Artistry of Compatibility
The target machine architecture and instruction set form
the canvas on which the art of code generation is
painted. A deep understanding of these architectural
elements is fundamental for a compiler to produce
efficient, correct, and compatible machine code. As we
venture further into the world of code generation, we will
explore advanced techniques, optimizations, and code
generation strategies that harmonize source code with
the intricacies of diverse target architectures, ensuring
the creation of efficient and performant executables.

III. Register Allocation and Management
Orchestrating the Symphony of Execution
In the intricate composition of code generation, register
allocation and management play the role of the
conductor, orchestrating the symphony of execution.
This chapter explores the art and science of efficiently

managing registers—the fast, limited storage within the CPU—ensuring that they are put to the most effective use during code generation.

Registers: The Virtuoso Performers
Registers are the virtuoso performers of a processor, capable of lightning-fast data access and manipulation. They are the heart of the CPU's execution engine, allowing instructions to operate on data with minimal latency. However, registers are a finite and precious resource, and efficient register allocation is vital to maximize a program's performance.

Understanding Register Allocation: The Score of Efficiency
Register allocation is the process of deciding which variables and temporary values should reside in registers during a program's execution. Its goal is to minimize memory access, optimize instruction scheduling, and enhance the program's execution speed. Here's a deeper look at register allocation:

1. Register File: The register file is the collection of registers available to a processor. It typically includes general-purpose registers (GPRs) and, on some architectures, special-purpose registers (e.g., floating-point registers or SIMD registers).

2. Register Constraints: Different processor architectures impose constraints on register usage. These constraints may include the number of available registers, their usage conventions (e.g., callee-saved and caller-saved registers), and operand restrictions.

3. Variables and Values: During program execution, variables and temporary values must reside in registers for computation. Register allocation determines which

variables are allocated to registers and when they are loaded from and stored to memory.

4. Lifetime Analysis: Register allocation involves analyzing the lifetime of variables, i.e., the intervals during which their values are needed. Variables with longer lifetimes are more likely to benefit from residing in registers.

5. Spilling: When there are more variables than available registers, some variables may be "spilled" to memory temporarily. Spilling involves storing a variable's value in memory and reloading it when needed. Spilling can introduce additional memory access overhead.

Register Allocation Strategies: The Conductor's Baton Efficient register allocation strategies are the conductor's baton that guides the orchestra of execution. Here are some common strategies used in register allocation:

1. Graph Coloring: This strategy models register allocation as a graph-coloring problem, where variables are nodes in the graph, and edges represent conflicts (variables that cannot share the same register). The goal is to assign colors (registers) to nodes such that no two adjacent nodes have the same color.

2. Linear Scan: Linear scan is a simple and efficient register allocation strategy. It scans through variables in the order they are encountered in the code and allocates registers until they are exhausted. When registers run out, it may spill variables to memory.

3. Live-Range Splitting: Live-range splitting divides a long-lived variable's range into smaller, more manageable segments. This strategy can help reduce the need for spilling and improve register allocation.

4. Interference Graph: Interference graph-based strategies build a graph representing variable interference. Nodes in the graph represent variables, and edges represent interference between variables. Techniques like graph coloring are then applied to allocate registers.

5. Register Pressure Analysis: Register pressure analysis assesses the demand for registers at various program points. It guides register allocation decisions by favoring variables with higher register pressure for allocation.

Spill Code Generation: When spilling occurs, the code generator generates instructions to spill values from registers to memory and reload them when needed. This code generation process must be efficient to minimize the performance impact of spilling.

Conclusion: The Symphony of Efficiency
Register allocation and management are the conductors in the symphony of execution, ensuring that registers are allocated and utilized efficiently during code generation. An optimal allocation strategy can significantly impact a program's performance by reducing memory access and enhancing instruction scheduling. As we proceed into the realm of code generation, we will explore advanced register allocation techniques, optimizations, and considerations that fine-tune the orchestration, ensuring that programs execute with the precision and efficiency of a well-conducted symphony.

IV. Handling Memory and Data Layout
The Art of Spatial Composition
In the grand composition of code generation, the orchestration of memory and data layout is akin to the spatial arrangement of instruments in an orchestra. This chapter delves into the intricacies of managing memory

and data layout—an essential aspect of code generation that directly impacts a program's efficiency and performance.

Memory and Data: The Canvas of Execution

Memory is the canvas on which a program's data is stored, retrieved, and manipulated. Efficient memory and data layout are crucial for optimizing data access patterns, minimizing memory latency, and ensuring that the orchestra of execution plays harmoniously.

Understanding Memory and Data Layout: The Spatial Composition

Memory and data layout refer to how data is organized and positioned in memory during program execution. This includes the arrangement of variables, data structures, and code segments in memory. Key aspects of memory and data layout include:

1. Data Types and Alignment: Different data types (e.g., integers, floating-point numbers, structures) have specific memory requirements and alignment constraints. Efficient data layout ensures that data elements are stored in memory according to these constraints.

2. Data Structures: Complex data structures, such as arrays, linked lists, trees, and hash tables, require careful consideration of memory layout to optimize access patterns. This includes minimizing cache misses and reducing memory fragmentation.

3. Memory Allocation: Memory allocation strategies, such as stack allocation and heap allocation, affect the layout of data in memory. Stack allocation is typically used for function call frames and local variables, while heap allocation is for dynamically allocated data.

4. Data Layout for Caching: Modern processors rely on hierarchical memory systems, including caches. Efficient data layout aims to maximize cache utilization by organizing data in a way that minimizes cache misses.

5. Code and Data Segmentation: In some architectures, code and data are stored in separate memory segments. Code generation must adhere to these segmentation rules.

Memory Hierarchy: The Layers of Sound
Memory is organized in a hierarchical structure that includes registers, caches, main memory, and secondary storage. Efficient memory and data layout aim to minimize the time it takes to access data by optimizing its placement within this hierarchy.

1. Registers: Registers are the fastest memory locations within the CPU. Efficient register allocation ensures that frequently used data resides in registers to minimize latency.

2. Cache: Caches sit between registers and main memory. Optimizing data layout for caching involves ensuring that frequently accessed data is present in cache lines to reduce memory access times.

3. Main Memory: Main memory is the primary storage location for program data. Memory layout must consider the organization of data in RAM to minimize access times.

4. Secondary Storage: Secondary storage includes devices like hard drives and SSDs. It's used for persistent data storage but has significantly higher access times than main memory. Efficient data layout can reduce the need for secondary storage access.

Data Alignment: The Musical Score
Data alignment is a crucial consideration in memory and data layout. Many architectures require data elements to be aligned in memory for efficient access. Misaligned data can result in performance penalties or even hardware exceptions.

Memory Layout Strategies: The Composer's Palette
Efficient memory and data layout involve employing various strategies to optimize data access patterns, minimize memory fragmentation, and reduce cache misses:

1. Struct of Arrays (SoA) vs. Array of Structs (AoS): SoA arranges data elements into separate arrays, optimizing cache utilization. AoS groups data elements together in structures, improving data locality.

2. Padding and Packing: Padding adds extra space to align data elements in memory. Packing eliminates unused space to reduce memory consumption. The choice depends on the balance between alignment and memory efficiency.

3. Data Structure Layout: Data structures like trees and linked lists benefit from careful arrangement of nodes in memory to minimize cache misses during traversal.

4. Cache Awareness: Cache-aware data layout aims to keep frequently accessed data together in memory, reducing cache misses.

5. Memory Segmentation: In some architectures, data is segmented into different memory areas with distinct access characteristics. Code generation must consider these segments when placing data.

Conclusion: The Spatial Symphony

Handling memory and data layout is the spatial composition of code generation. Efficiently orchestrating data in memory is essential for achieving optimal program performance. As we journey further into the world of code generation, we will explore advanced memory and data layout techniques, optimizations, and spatial considerations that empower compilers to create programs that execute with the harmony and precision of a well-arranged symphony.

V. Generating Machine Code from Intermediate Code

The Alchemy of Transformation

In the symphony of compiler construction, the transformation of intermediate code into machine code is akin to the alchemical transmutation of base elements into gold. This chapter delves into the intricate art and science of generating machine code from intermediate code—a process that bridges the realms of abstraction and execution, turning high-level intentions into tangible instructions.

The Bridge Between Abstraction and Execution: Intermediate Code

Intermediate code serves as the bridge between high-level programming languages and machine code. It provides a structured, language-independent representation of a program's logic, free from the idiosyncrasies of specific source languages or target architectures. During the code generation phase, this intermediate representation is transmuted into machine-executable instructions.

Understanding Intermediate Code: The Lingua Franca

Intermediate code is an abstract representation that simplifies complex program logic. It is characterized by the following traits:

1. Language Independence: Intermediate code is not bound to a specific programming language, making it a universal intermediary for diverse source languages.

2. Simplified Syntax: It typically has a simpler syntax, focusing on essential program structures and operations.

3. Abstraction of High-Level Constructs: Intermediate code abstracts high-level language constructs, such as loops and conditionals, into more basic building blocks.

4. Platform Agnostic: It is designed to be platform-agnostic, allowing the same intermediate code to be translated into machine code for different target architectures.

Machine Code Generation: The Alchemical Process
The generation of machine code from intermediate code is a meticulous process that involves several essential steps:

1. Instruction Selection: The first step is selecting appropriate machine instructions for each intermediate code operation. This involves mapping high-level language constructs to their corresponding machine instructions.

2. Register Allocation: The intermediate code specifies the use of temporary variables, and efficient register allocation determines which variables should reside in registers during execution.

3. Addressing Modes: Addressing modes dictate how memory operands are addressed in machine code. The code generator must translate intermediate code memory references into the appropriate addressing modes.

4. Control Flow Generation: Intermediate code represents control flow using high-level constructs like conditionals and loops. The code generator transforms these constructs into machine code instructions, such as conditional branches and jumps.

5. Data Layout: Data layout is crucial for efficient memory access. The code generator must ensure that data elements are correctly positioned in memory to optimize data access patterns.

6. Error Handling: The code generator must handle error conditions that may arise during code generation, such as invalid operations or unsupported constructs.

Target Architecture Considerations: The Alchemical Philosopher's Stone
The target machine architecture plays a central role in machine code generation. Different architectures have unique instruction sets, addressing modes, and memory layouts, necessitating target-specific code generation strategies.

1. Instruction Encoding: The code generator must produce machine code instructions in the correct format and encoding for the target architecture.

2. Register Mapping: It must map intermediate code variables and temporary values to the target machine's registers, adhering to its register conventions.

3. Memory Organization: Data and code segments must be placed in memory according to the target architecture's organization, including segment boundaries and addressing limitations.

4. Endianness: The code generator must account for endianness, ensuring that multi-byte data is stored and accessed correctly in memory.

Optimizations in Code Generation: The Elixir of Performance

During machine code generation, the code generator may apply various optimizations to improve the efficiency and performance of the resulting code. These optimizations may include constant folding, common subexpression elimination, and peephole optimizations, among others.

Conclusion: The Alchemical Mastery

The generation of machine code from intermediate code is the alchemical process that transmutes high-level intentions into executable instructions. It requires a deep understanding of both the target architecture and the intricacies of the intermediate code representation. As we delve further into the world of code generation, we will explore advanced techniques, optimizations, and target-specific considerations that empower compilers to master this alchemical art, ensuring the creation of efficient and performant machine code from the crucible of intermediate representations.

V. Generating Machine Code from Intermediate Code (Reiterated)

The Final Alchemy

In the grand symphony of compiler construction, the transformation of intermediate code into machine code is the crescendo—the final, alchemical step that transforms abstract program representations into the concrete instructions that a computer's processor can execute. This chapter explores the intricate art and science of generating machine code from intermediate code—a process that lies at the heart of a compiler's mission.

Intermediate Code: The Bridge Between Worlds
Intermediate code is the lingua franca of compilers, serving as an intermediary representation that simplifies complex high-level code into a structured, platform-agnostic format. It encapsulates the essential logic of a program, free from the syntactical quirks and language-specific idiosyncrasies.

The Role of Intermediate Code:

1. Language Independence: Intermediate code transcends the constraints of any specific programming language, making it a versatile conduit for translating diverse source languages into machine code.

2. Abstraction of High-Level Constructs: It abstracts away the intricacies of high-level language constructs, breaking them down into their fundamental operations.

3. Simplification: By providing a simplified representation, intermediate code eases the challenges of translation and optimization, enabling the code generator to focus on core logic.

Machine Code Generation: Crafting the Art
The generation of machine code from intermediate code is a meticulous craft that requires a profound understanding of both the intermediate representation and the target architecture. This process comprises several fundamental steps:

1. Instruction Selection: The code generator maps each operation in the intermediate code to the appropriate machine code instruction. This involves choosing the correct opcode and operand formats to faithfully represent the high-level intent.

2. Register Allocation: Efficient register allocation determines which intermediate code variables and temporary values should reside in processor registers during execution. It aims to minimize memory access, enhance instruction scheduling, and optimize execution speed.

3. Addressing Modes: The code generator must translate intermediate code memory references into the appropriate addressing modes for the target architecture. Addressing modes dictate how operands are accessed in memory, including direct addressing, indirect addressing, and indexed addressing.

4. Control Flow Generation: Intermediate code often employs high-level control structures such as conditionals and loops. The code generator transforms these constructs into machine code instructions for conditional branches, jumps, and subroutine calls, ensuring the correct flow of execution.

5. Data Layout: Efficient data layout is vital for optimizing memory access patterns. The code generator arranges data elements in memory to minimize cache misses and reduce memory latency.

6. Error Handling: Robust error handling within the code generator addresses unexpected conditions during code generation, such as unsupported constructs or invalid operations.

Target Architecture Considerations: The Architect's Blueprint
Each target architecture is unique, with its own instruction set, addressing modes, and memory organization. The code generator must take these architectural nuances into account:

1. Instruction Encoding: Machine code instructions must conform to the target architecture's encoding scheme, adhering to specific opcode formats and operand requirements.

2. Register Mapping: Intermediate code variables and temporary values must be mapped to the target architecture's registers, following register conventions and usage guidelines.

3. Memory Organization: Data and code segments must be placed in memory according to the target architecture's organization, respecting segment boundaries and alignment requirements.

4. Endianness: The code generator must handle endianness, ensuring that multi-byte data is correctly stored and accessed in memory.

Optimizations in Code Generation: Enhancing the Performance

The code generator can apply various optimizations during machine code generation to enhance performance. These optimizations may include constant folding, common subexpression elimination, and peephole optimizations, among others. Their goal is to produce efficient and streamlined machine code.

Conclusion: The Culmination of the Compiler's Journey

Generating machine code from intermediate code is the culmination of a compiler's journey, where high-level abstractions transform into executable instructions. It is an intricate art that demands a profound understanding of both the intermediate representation and the target architecture. As we advance deeper into the realm of code generation, we will explore advanced techniques, optimizations, and target-specific considerations that empower compilers to master this final alchemy, ensuring the creation of efficient and high-performing machine code from the fertile ground of intermediate representations.

VI. Code Generation for Different Processor Architectures

The Multilingual Compiler

In the symphony of code generation, crafting machine code for different processor architectures is akin to conducting a multilingual orchestra. This chapter explores the intricate art and science of generating code that harmonizes with the diverse dialects spoken by various processor architectures—a process that showcases the compiler's adaptability and mastery.

Processor Architectures: The Languages of Machines
Processor architectures are the languages of machines, each with its own grammar, vocabulary, and nuances. These architectures define the instruction set, memory hierarchy, addressing modes, and execution behavior that compilers must understand and respect. Common processor architectures include x86, ARM, MIPS, PowerPC, and more.

The Challenge of Multilingual Code Generation:

1. Instruction Sets: Each architecture has a unique instruction set that specifies the operations it can perform. Compilers must select the appropriate instructions to execute high-level language constructs.

2. Registers: The number, types, and usage conventions of registers vary among architectures. Register allocation strategies must align with the target architecture's register resources.

3. Memory Hierarchy: Architectures differ in their memory hierarchies, cache sizes, and memory access

patterns. Code generators must optimize data layout to minimize cache misses.

4. Endianness: Some architectures use big-endian byte order, while others use little-endian. Compilers must ensure that data is stored and accessed correctly.

5. Addressing Modes: Addressing modes dictate how memory operands are accessed. Compilers must generate code that adheres to the addressing modes supported by the target architecture.

Architecture-Aware Code Generation: The Polyglot Compiler

Code generation for different processor architectures requires a polyglot approach. The compiler must adapt its output to the idiosyncrasies of each architecture while maintaining high-level language semantics. Key considerations include:

1. Instruction Selection: The code generator selects the appropriate machine instructions for each high-level operation. It must map language constructs to the target architecture's instruction set, considering factors like operand types and addressing modes.

2. Register Allocation: Register allocation strategies adapt to the number and types of registers available on the target architecture. The code generator aims to minimize memory access by efficiently using registers.

3. Addressing Mode Translation: Memory references in intermediate code are translated into the target architecture's addressing modes, which may include direct, indexed, or register-indirect addressing.

4. Code Scheduling: Instruction scheduling is influenced by the target architecture's pipelining and execution

units. The code generator organizes instructions to exploit parallelism and minimize pipeline stalls.

5. Memory Layout: Data and code segments must be positioned in memory according to the target architecture's memory organization, including segment boundaries, alignment requirements, and cache optimizations.

Optimizations for Specific Architectures: The Dialect of Performance
Optimizations can be tailored to specific architectures, leveraging their unique features:

1. SIMD Optimization: For architectures with SIMD (Single Instruction, Multiple Data) capabilities, compilers can vectorize code to exploit parallelism.

2. Fused Instructions: Some architectures support fused instructions that perform multiple operations in a single instruction. Compilers can generate code to take advantage of these features.

3. Hardware-Specific Instructions: Target-specific optimizations can use architecture-specific instructions or features to enhance performance.

4. Memory Hierarchy Awareness: Compilers can optimize data layout to reduce cache misses, taking into account the target architecture's cache size and associativity.

Cross-Compilation and Portability: The Bilingual Compiler
Cross-compilers are capable of generating code for a target architecture different from the one on which the compiler itself runs. This feature is essential for

producing software for embedded systems, mobile devices, and other platforms.

Conclusion: The Multilingual Maestro
Code generation for different processor architectures is the symphony of the multilingual compiler. It requires a deep understanding of each architecture's language and a mastery of adaptation. As we delve further into the world of code generation, we will explore advanced techniques, optimizations, and architectural considerations that empower compilers to conduct this multilingual orchestra, ensuring that code resonates harmoniously with the diverse dialects of the computing world.

Chapter 8: Run-Time Systems

I. Run-Time Systems
The Silent Guardians of Executable Harmony
In the grand narrative of compilers, once the baton of code generation is lowered, the spotlight shifts to the performers—the compiled programs. Yet, behind the scenes, an ensemble of critical components and services works tirelessly to ensure the seamless execution of these programs. This chapter explores the profound role of run-time systems—a silent orchestra that enables the harmonious performance of compiled programs.

The Silent Guardians: Run-Time Systems Defined
Run-time systems encompass a constellation of software and services that accompany compiled programs during their execution. These systems provide essential support for program execution, handling tasks that range from memory management to dynamic linking and exception handling. They are an integral part of the runtime environment in which a program operates.

Understanding Run-Time Systems: The Ensemble of Services
Run-time systems encompass a wide range of services that support program execution:

1. Memory Management: Run-time systems manage the allocation and deallocation of memory for program data and stack frames. This includes stack memory for function calls and heap memory for dynamically allocated data.

2. Type Information: They store and manage type information, enabling runtime type checking and casting. This is particularly important in languages with dynamic typing.

3. Garbage Collection: In languages that use automatic memory management, run-time systems employ garbage collection algorithms to reclaim memory occupied by objects that are no longer in use.

4. Dynamic Linking: Run-time systems facilitate dynamic linking, allowing programs to access libraries and external functions during execution. This enables modular code and reduces executable file sizes.

5. Exception Handling: They provide mechanisms for handling exceptions and runtime errors, ensuring that programs can gracefully recover from unexpected situations.

6. Thread Management: In multi-threaded programs, run-time systems manage threads, including their creation, synchronization, and termination.

7. I/O Operations: They facilitate input and output operations, ensuring that programs can interact with external devices, files, and networks.

8. Virtual Machines: In some environments, run-time systems employ virtual machines to execute bytecode or intermediate code, adding an additional layer of abstraction for platform independence.

Run-Time Libraries: The Score of Harmony
Run-time systems often rely on run-time libraries— collections of precompiled code modules that provide common functionality. These libraries include the Standard Library for a given programming language, which offers a range of functions and data structures to simplify common tasks.

Dynamic Linking and Loading: The Scene Changes

Dynamic linking and loading are essential components of run-time systems. They enable programs to access external libraries and functions at runtime, reducing memory usage and promoting code reuse. When a program is executed, the operating system's dynamic linker loads the necessary libraries into memory and resolves references to external functions.

Dynamic Memory Allocation and Garbage Collection: The Maestros of Memory

Memory management is a critical function of run-time systems. Dynamic memory allocation allows programs to request memory from the system at runtime, while garbage collection ensures that memory occupied by unreferenced objects is reclaimed. The choice of memory management strategy, such as reference counting or tracing garbage collection, depends on the programming language and the run-time system's design.

Exception Handling: The Safety Net

Exception handling mechanisms provided by run-time systems enable programs to gracefully handle errors and exceptional conditions. Whether it's a null reference, a division by zero, or an out-of-bounds array access, these mechanisms help prevent crashes and enable controlled error recovery.

Conclusion: The Unseen Guardians

Run-time systems are the unseen guardians of executable harmony, working behind the curtains to ensure that compiled programs perform seamlessly. They handle memory, types, exceptions, dynamic linking, and much more, allowing programs to run safely and efficiently. As we delve deeper into the world of run-time systems, we will uncover the intricacies of memory management, dynamic loading, and exception handling, gaining a deeper appreciation for the essential role they play in the execution of compiled code.

II. Memory Management
The Art of Allocating and Organizing Space
Memory management is one of the core functions of a run-time system, and it plays a pivotal role in the execution of compiled programs. It involves the allocation and organization of memory to store program data, stack frames, and dynamically allocated objects. Memory management decisions impact program efficiency, stability, and resource utilization, making it a crucial topic for understanding the inner workings of run-time systems.

Memory in the Runtime Environment: A Precious Resource
Memory in the runtime environment is akin to a finite, precious resource. Efficient memory management aims to use this resource judiciously while ensuring that programs can execute without running out of memory or causing memory-related errors.

Memory Segmentation: The Landscape of Memory
In the runtime environment, memory is typically divided into distinct segments:

1. Code Segment: This segment stores the compiled machine code of the program. It is typically marked as read-only to prevent unintended modifications.

2. Data Segment: The data segment holds global and static variables. These variables have a fixed memory location for the entire program's execution.

3. Stack Segment: The stack segment is used for managing function call frames and local variables. It

operates as a Last-In-First-Out (LIFO) data structure, and each function call creates a new stack frame.

4. Heap Segment: The heap segment is reserved for dynamically allocated data. It is a region of memory where objects are allocated and deallocated as needed during program execution.

Stack Allocation: The Call and Return
Stack allocation is a memory management strategy where memory for local variables and function call frames is allocated on a stack data structure. This stack is known as the call stack or execution stack.

Key Aspects of Stack Allocation:

1. Local Variables: Local variables declared within a function are typically allocated on the stack. Each function call creates a new stack frame, which includes space for its local variables.

2. Function Calls and Returns: The stack is used to manage the call and return sequence of function executions. When a function is called, a new stack frame is pushed onto the stack. When the function returns, its stack frame is popped, deallocating the associated memory.

3. Automatic Storage Duration: Memory allocated on the stack has automatic storage duration, meaning it is automatically deallocated when the function execution scope ends.

4. Deterministic Memory Management: Stack allocation follows a deterministic pattern, making it relatively straightforward to manage memory. However, it has limited flexibility for dynamic memory allocation.

Heap Allocation: Dynamic Memory on Demand
Heap allocation is a memory management strategy that allows for the dynamic allocation and deallocation of memory during program execution. It provides a flexible and dynamic memory pool for objects whose size or lifetime cannot be determined at compile time.

Key Aspects of Heap Allocation:

1. Dynamic Memory Requests: Programs can request memory from the heap at runtime using functions like `malloc` or `new` in languages like C or C++. This memory remains allocated until explicitly freed.

2. Manual Deallocation: Unlike stack memory, heap memory must be manually deallocated using functions like `free` or `delete`. Failure to deallocate can result in memory leaks.

3. Variable Lifetime: Objects allocated on the heap can have variable lifetimes, depending on when they are explicitly deallocated. This flexibility is essential for managing objects with unpredictable lifetimes.

4. Memory Fragmentation: Over time, heap memory can become fragmented, leading to inefficient memory usage. Memory allocators attempt to mitigate fragmentation to maintain efficient memory utilization.

Choosing the Right Allocation: The Balance of Trade-offs
The choice between stack and heap allocation depends on various factors, including the lifetime, scope, and size of objects:

1. Stack Allocation: Ideal for short-lived, local variables and function call frames. It offers deterministic memory management but has limited flexibility for dynamic memory allocation.

2. Heap Allocation: Suited for objects with variable lifetimes, dynamic memory requirements, and objects that must persist beyond the scope of a single function. It offers flexibility but requires manual memory management.

Conclusion: The Memory Maestros
Memory management is a fundamental aspect of run-time systems, ensuring that programs can efficiently allocate and use memory resources. Stack allocation is well-suited for local variables and function call management, while heap allocation provides flexibility for dynamic memory needs. Understanding these memory management strategies is crucial for writing efficient and robust software and appreciating the role run-time systems play in executing compiled programs.

III. Run-Time Libraries
The Silent Enablers of Program Functionality
In the intricate symphony of software execution, run-time libraries are the virtuoso performers that ensure the harmony of a compiled program's operation. These libraries consist of precompiled code modules that provide essential functions and routines, saving programmers from reinventing the wheel for common tasks. This section explores the world of run-time libraries, uncovering their functions and the vital role they play in the seamless execution of compiled programs.

Defining Run-Time Libraries: The Pillars of Functionality
Run-time libraries are collections of precompiled code modules and functions that are linked to compiled programs at runtime. They serve as a reservoir of reusable code, offering a range of essential functions and services, thereby reducing code redundancy and simplifying the development process.

Functions and Services Offered by Run-Time Libraries:

1. Input/Output Operations: Run-time libraries provide functions for reading from and writing to files, standard input, and standard output. These functions enable programs to interact with external data sources and users.

2. Memory Management: Memory allocation and deallocation functions, such as `malloc`, `free`, `calloc`, and `realloc`, are part of run-time libraries. They help manage dynamic memory usage, enhancing program efficiency and stability.

3. String Manipulation: Functions for manipulating strings, such as `strcpy`, `strcat`, `strlen`, and `strcmp`, simplify common string operations. These functions reduce the risk of buffer overflows and enhance code readability.

4. Mathematical Operations: Run-time libraries include mathematical functions like `sin`, `cos`, `sqrt`, and `pow`. These functions provide a wide range of mathematical operations for numerical computations.

5. Time and Date: Functions for working with time and date, such as `time`, `ctime`, and `strftime`, assist in tasks like timestamping, scheduling, and time-sensitive operations.

6. Dynamic Memory Management: Memory management functions, such as `malloc` and `free`, enable dynamic memory allocation and deallocation, supporting data structures like linked lists and trees.

7. File Handling: Libraries offer functions for opening, closing, reading, and writing files. These functions help

programs interact with the file system, manage configuration files, and perform file-based operations.

8. Error Handling: Libraries provide functions for error reporting and handling, allowing programs to detect and respond to unexpected conditions gracefully.

9. Localization and Internationalization: Functions for localization and internationalization enable software to adapt to different languages and regions, facilitating global software distribution.

10. Data Serialization: Libraries often include functions for serializing and deserializing data, making it easier to store and transmit structured data efficiently.

11. Networking: For networked applications, run-time libraries offer functions for socket programming, enabling communication over the internet or local networks.

12. User Interface: In graphical applications, libraries provide tools for creating graphical user interfaces, including windows, buttons, and input fields.

Linking Run-Time Libraries: The Symphony of Integration
When a program is compiled, the compiler links the necessary run-time libraries to the executable. There are two primary methods of linking run-time libraries:

1. Static Linking: In static linking, the necessary library code is included directly in the executable at compile time. This results in a self-contained executable file but can increase its size.

2. Dynamic Linking: With dynamic linking, the program references external library files at runtime. This reduces

executable size but requires the presence of the required libraries on the system where the program runs.

Custom Run-Time Libraries: Composing Unique Melodies

In addition to standard run-time libraries, developers can create custom libraries tailored to the specific needs of their applications. These custom libraries encapsulate functions and routines unique to the program, promoting code reuse and maintainability.

Conclusion: The Unsung Heroes

Run-time libraries are the unsung heroes of software execution, providing a wealth of functionality that empowers programmers to build complex applications efficiently. They offer essential functions for input/output, memory management, string manipulation, mathematics, and more. Understanding these libraries' capabilities and integrating them effectively is essential for writing robust, feature-rich, and maintainable software—a testament to the symbiotic relationship between compilers, run-time systems, and the libraries that bring code to life.

IV. Exception Handling and Runtime Error Reporting

The Safety Nets of Program Execution

In the complex choreography of program execution, exception handling and runtime error reporting serve as the safety nets that prevent the graceful ballet of software from descending into chaos. These mechanisms are indispensable components of run-time systems, providing the means to detect, manage, and recover from unexpected situations and errors that may arise during program execution. This section delves into the intricacies of exception handling and runtime error reporting, shedding light on their pivotal roles in ensuring the stability and reliability of compiled programs.

Exception Handling: The Safety Net for Unforeseen Events

Exception handling is a fundamental feature of many programming languages and run-time systems. It enables programs to respond gracefully to exceptional or unexpected conditions, often referred to as exceptions. These conditions can range from division by zero and null pointer dereferences to out-of-memory errors and file-not-found situations.

Key Components of Exception Handling:

1. Throwing Exceptions: In the event of an exceptional condition, a program can raise or "throw" an exception. This indicates that an error or abnormal situation has occurred.

2. Catching Exceptions: To manage exceptions, programs can employ "catch" blocks or exception handlers. These blocks specify how to handle particular types of exceptions when they are thrown.

3. Exception Types: Exceptions are often categorized into different types or classes, each representing a specific kind of error. This classification allows for fine-grained control over exception handling.

4. Propagation: Exceptions can propagate up the call stack if they are not caught immediately. This allows higher-level code to handle errors that lower-level code may not be equipped to address.

Runtime Error Reporting: Detecting and Diagnosing Issues

Runtime error reporting is a complementary mechanism that focuses on detecting and diagnosing errors during program execution. It includes the reporting of unexpected situations, such as invalid input, invalid state, or resource exhaustion, that do not necessarily lead to exceptions but still require attention.

Key Aspects of Runtime Error Reporting:

1. Error Codes: Programs often use error codes or error return values to signal issues during function or method calls. These codes are checked by the calling code to determine if an error has occurred.

2. Error Messages: Alongside error codes, error messages provide detailed information about the nature of the problem. These messages assist developers in diagnosing and resolving issues.

3. Logging: Logging is a common practice in runtime error reporting. It involves recording information about errors, warnings, and other events in log files. Log files help diagnose issues in deployed software.

4. Assert Statements: Assert statements are used to check conditions that are expected to be true at specific points in the program. If an assertion fails, it indicates a critical error, and the program typically terminates or raises an exception.

5. Resource Tracking: Resource tracking mechanisms monitor resource usage (e.g., memory, file handles) to detect resource leaks or excessive consumption.

Exception Handling vs. Runtime Error Reporting: A Dual Approach
Exception handling and runtime error reporting complement each other in ensuring the reliability of software:

- Exception handling is suitable for dealing with exceptional conditions that may occur but are not always erroneous, such as user input validation.

- Runtime error reporting focuses on detecting and diagnosing issues that do not necessarily lead to exceptions but still require attention, such as resource exhaustion.

The Art of Recovery: Graceful Degradation and Error Handling Strategies
Effective exception handling and runtime error reporting not only detect issues but also define strategies for recovery or graceful degradation. These strategies may include:

1. Retry Mechanisms: Attempting the operation again after a transient error.

2. Fallback Mechanisms: Switching to alternative methods or approaches when the primary one fails.

3. Error Propagation: Escalating the error to higher-level components for handling.

4. Graceful Termination: Terminating the program gracefully, ensuring that resources are released and no data loss occurs.

5. Logging and Reporting: Recording error details for debugging and future analysis.

Conclusion: The Safety Nets of Software Ballet
Exception handling and runtime error reporting are the safety nets that ensure the graceful execution of compiled programs. They provide the means to detect, manage, and recover from unexpected conditions, errors, and issues that may arise during program

execution. By adopting robust error-handling practices and strategies, programmers can enhance the reliability, stability, and maintainability of their software, transforming it into a well-choreographed ballet that gracefully navigates the complexities of the computing stage.

V. Garbage Collection Techniques
Taming the Memory Jungle
In the intricate dance of program execution, memory management takes center stage, and at its heart lies the art of garbage collection. This essential function within run-time systems orchestrates the reclamation of memory no longer in use, ensuring that programs maintain peak performance without memory leaks or resource exhaustion. This section explores the diverse techniques employed in garbage collection, revealing the methods that maintain the delicate balance between memory efficiency and program stability.

The Memory Challenge: Allocation vs. Deallocation
In the realm of memory management, the allocation and deallocation of memory are two sides of the same coin. Memory must be allocated to store data and structures during program execution, but it must also be systematically and efficiently deallocated to prevent memory leaks and resource wastage. This delicate equilibrium is where garbage collection comes into play.

The Garbage Collection Challenge: Identifying Unreachable Objects
The primary objective of garbage collection is to identify and reclaim memory occupied by objects that are no longer reachable or accessible by the program. These objects may be abandoned due to the cessation of references to them or because they exist in a scope that has concluded. The challenge is to differentiate between

objects that are still in use and those that have become "garbage."

Common Garbage Collection Techniques:

1. Reference Counting: Reference counting tracks the number of references to each object. When an object's reference count drops to zero, it is considered garbage and can be safely deallocated. While simple and predictable, reference counting struggles with cyclic references and can result in resource leaks.

2. Mark-and-Sweep: The mark-and-sweep algorithm divides memory into two regions: the heap and the free list. It identifies and marks all live objects (those still reachable) and sweeps away unmarked objects, returning their memory to the free list. This technique is robust but can introduce fragmentation.

3. Generational Garbage Collection: This approach recognizes that most objects become unreachable shortly after allocation. It divides the heap into generations, promoting objects that survive collection to older generations. Younger generations are collected more frequently, while older ones are collected less often. This strategy leverages the observation that younger objects tend to die quickly, reducing the overhead of scanning long-lived objects.

4. Copying Garbage Collection: The copying collector divides memory into two halves: the "from" space and the "to" space. Live objects are copied from the "from" space to the "to" space during collection. This approach eliminates fragmentation and can be combined with generational collection for efficiency.

5. Reference Counting with Cycle Detection: Combining reference counting with cycle detection helps mitigate

issues with cyclic references. It identifies and collects objects that are part of reference cycles by periodically running cycle detection algorithms.

6. Concurrent Garbage Collection: Concurrent garbage collection minimizes pauses by allowing the collector to run concurrently with the application. This approach is essential for applications with strict real-time requirements or those that must maintain high responsiveness.

The Challenge of Choosing the Right Technique: Balancing Act
Selecting the most suitable garbage collection technique is a delicate balancing act that depends on several factors, including the programming language, application type, performance goals, and system constraints. A real-time embedded system may opt for a different strategy than a web server handling thousands of concurrent connections.

Conclusion: Harmonizing Memory and Performance
Garbage collection is the conductor of the memory management orchestra, ensuring that memory is allocated and deallocated efficiently. These techniques strike a balance between memory efficiency and program stability. Understanding the strengths and weaknesses of various garbage collection methods empowers developers to make informed choices, orchestrating the memory dance that allows programs to perform seamlessly, gracefully navigating the intricacies of memory management.

VI. Just-in-Time (JIT) Compilation
The Art of Dynamic Code Generation
In the realm of program execution, the concept of "just-in-time" (JIT) compilation represents a dynamic and transformative process that bridges the gap between

source code and machine code. JIT compilation is a key feature of run-time systems, offering a unique set of advantages that combine the flexibility of interpreted languages with the performance of compiled languages. This section explores JIT compilation, shedding light on its mechanisms and the myriad benefits it brings to the world of computing.

The Nature of Compilation: Ahead-of-Time vs. Just-in-Time
Traditionally, program execution occurs through an ahead-of-time (AOT) compilation process. In AOT, source code is translated into machine code by the compiler before execution. The result is a standalone executable file that can be run independently. While AOT compilation offers excellent performance, it lacks the adaptability and dynamism required for certain scenarios.

The JIT Compilation Paradigm: Dynamic Code Generation on Demand
JIT compilation flips the script, introducing dynamic code generation during program execution. Instead of translating the entire program to machine code before execution, JIT compilation translates code fragments, or even individual functions, at runtime, precisely when they are needed.

Key Advantages of JIT Compilation:

1. Improved Performance: JIT compilation optimizes code for the specific execution environment, taking into account runtime information. This results in code that can be highly tailored for the target platform, often surpassing the performance of statically compiled code.

2. Reduced Memory Footprint: Because only the necessary code is compiled as needed, JIT-compiled

programs can have smaller memory footprints compared to their statically compiled counterparts. This is particularly advantageous in resource-constrained environments.

3. Adaptability and Portability: JIT-compiled programs can adapt to the specific characteristics of the runtime environment, making them highly portable across different platforms and architectures. This adaptability is particularly valuable in cross-platform development.

4. Late Binding: JIT compilation allows for late binding of code, enabling features like dynamic linking and runtime class loading. This is essential for scenarios where code modules need to be loaded and executed dynamically.

5. Dynamic Optimization: JIT compilers can apply dynamic optimization techniques, such as inlining, loop unrolling, and constant folding, based on the actual usage patterns of the program. This results in highly efficient code execution.

6. Reflection and Metaprogramming: JIT compilation can facilitate advanced programming techniques like reflection and metaprogramming by allowing the generation and execution of code at runtime based on program state and data.

7. Hotspot Detection: JIT compilers can identify "hotspots" in the code—sections of code that are frequently executed. They can then prioritize the compilation of these hotspots for maximum performance gains.

8. Enhanced Security: By compiling code on-demand, JIT compilers can incorporate security checks and access controls dynamically, making it harder for malicious code to exploit vulnerabilities.

JIT Compilation in Action: Dynamic Code Generation
The JIT compilation process generally involves the following steps:

1. Parsing and Lexing: The source code is parsed and lexed to generate an abstract syntax tree (AST).

2. Intermediate Representation (IR): The AST is transformed into an intermediate representation (IR) that is closer to the target machine code but still abstract enough for optimization.

3. Optimization: The IR is optimized to improve performance. Common optimizations include dead code elimination, constant folding, and loop unrolling.

4. Code Generation: The optimized IR is translated into machine code specific to the execution environment.

5. Execution: The generated machine code is executed as needed, with the option to further optimize and recompile frequently executed code paths.

Conclusion: Bridging the Gap Between Flexibility and Performance
Just-in-time (JIT) compilation is a remarkable innovation in the world of program execution, seamlessly combining the adaptability of interpreted languages with the performance of statically compiled languages. By dynamically generating machine code on demand, JIT compilers achieve exceptional performance, reduce memory overhead, enhance portability, and enable advanced programming techniques. This dynamic code generation approach exemplifies the synergy between compilation and runtime, allowing programs to perform at their peak while navigating the ever-evolving landscape of computing environments.

Chapter 9: Compiler Frontends and Backends

I. Overview of Compiler Frontends and Backends

The Dual Essence of Compilation

The process of transforming human-readable source code into machine-executable instructions is a multifaceted endeavor that compilers undertake with remarkable precision and complexity. At the core of this journey lie two distinct yet intimately connected components: the frontend and the backend. In this chapter, we embark on a journey through the intricacies of compiler construction, dissecting the roles and responsibilities of these two essential halves and appreciating their harmonious collaboration.

The Frontend: Bridging Human and Machine Languages
The frontend of a compiler is the first point of contact between a programmer and the compilation process. Its primary mission is to understand, analyze, and process the high-level source code provided by the programmer. Let's explore the crucial functions performed by the frontend:

1. Lexical Analysis: The process begins with lexical analysis or scanning, where the source code is broken down into tokens, the smallest syntactic units like keywords, identifiers, and literals. This step involves recognizing the language's grammar rules and identifying the lexemes within the source code.

2. Syntax Analysis (Parsing): The next step is syntax analysis or parsing. Here, the compiler verifies that the source code adheres to the language's syntax rules, creating an abstract syntax tree (AST) or a similar intermediate representation that captures the code's structure and relationships between elements.

3. Semantic Analysis: After parsing, semantic analysis comes into play. This phase checks the source code for semantic correctness, ensuring that variable types, function signatures, and expressions follow the language's rules. Semantic analysis helps catch errors that may not be apparent from the syntax alone.

4. Intermediate Code Generation: Some compilers generate an intermediate representation (IR) at this stage. The IR is a bridge between the high-level source code and the machine code, simplifying subsequent optimization and code generation phases.

5. Error Handling: Throughout the frontend process, the compiler must provide meaningful error messages and diagnostics to aid the programmer in identifying and correcting issues in the source code.

The Backend: Transforming High-Level Abstractions into Machine Code
Once the frontend has diligently processed and verified the source code, the backend takes over, translating the high-level abstractions into machine code that can be executed by the target hardware. The backend is responsible for a series of intricate tasks:

1. Optimization: The optimization phase seeks to improve the efficiency and performance of the generated code. Various optimization techniques, such as constant folding, common subexpression elimination, and loop optimization, are applied to the intermediate representation.

2. Code Generation: The heart of the backend is the code generation phase. Here, the compiler translates the optimized intermediate representation into machine code or assembly language specific to the target architecture.

This process involves mapping high-level constructs to low-level machine instructions.

3. Register Allocation: In this step, the compiler allocates registers to hold intermediate values and variables. Register allocation aims to minimize the use of memory locations, as accessing registers is significantly faster than accessing memory.

4. Instruction Scheduling: For processors with multiple execution units, instruction scheduling determines the order in which instructions are executed to maximize parallelism and minimize stalls.

5. Memory Management: The backend also deals with memory management, which includes managing stack frames for function calls and allocating memory for dynamically created objects, such as those created using `malloc` or `new`.

6. Linking: In cases where the program consists of multiple source files or modules, the backend may perform linking, which combines these separate pieces into a single executable or library.

Frontend and Backend Harmony: The Compilation Symphony
The frontend and backend of a compiler operate in harmony, each responsible for a distinct set of tasks, but working together seamlessly to bridge the gap between human-readable source code and machine-executable instructions. This orchestration between the two halves of compilation is what transforms abstract programming concepts into tangible, functioning software.

Conclusion: The Magic Behind the Curtain
Compiler frontend and backend components are the unsung heroes of the software development process,

responsible for translating our ideas and algorithms into efficient and reliable machine code. The frontend ensures that our high-level code is sound and correctly adheres to language rules, while the backend works its magic to optimize and generate efficient machine code tailored to the target architecture. Understanding this dual essence of compilation is key to appreciating the complexity and beauty of the compiler's art.

II. Frontend Responsibilities
The Keystone of Compilation

At the heart of every compiler lies the frontend, a vital component responsible for interpreting, validating, and structuring the high-level source code written by programmers. The frontend acts as the gatekeeper, ensuring that the code adheres to the language's rules and constraints before passing it on to the backend for transformation into machine code. In this section, we delve into the intricacies of the frontend, exploring its fundamental responsibilities, which encompass lexical analysis, syntax analysis (parsing), and semantic analysis.

1. Lexical Analysis: Parsing the Source Code into Tokens

The journey of compilation commences with lexical analysis, often referred to as scanning. This phase deals with the source code as a stream of characters, breaking it down into discrete units called tokens. Lexical analysis serves several crucial functions:

- Tokenization: The process begins with tokenization, where the source code is divided into meaningful units, such as keywords, identifiers, literals, operators, and punctuation. For example, in the statement `int x = 42;`, the tokens include `int`, `x`, `=`, and `42`.

- Ignoring Whitespace and Comments: Lexical analysis also involves discarding insignificant characters, such as whitespace and comments, which don't contribute to the code's logical structure.

- Error Detection: Lexical analysis is the first line of defense against syntax errors. It can catch misspelled keywords or malformed tokens, allowing for early error detection and helpful diagnostics.

- Creating a Symbol Table: The frontend often constructs a symbol table during lexical analysis to keep track of identifiers and their associated information, like data types and memory addresses. This symbol table becomes crucial during later phases of compilation.

2. Syntax Analysis (Parsing): Structuring the Code
With tokens in hand, the frontend proceeds to the syntax analysis phase, also known as parsing. Parsing involves analyzing the arrangement of tokens to create a structured representation of the code, typically in the form of an abstract syntax tree (AST) or a similar data structure. Key tasks during parsing include:

- Verifying Syntax Rules: The parser checks whether the code adheres to the language's syntax rules and grammar. It ensures that statements are properly structured and that expressions are well-formed.

- Building an AST: As it parses, the frontend constructs an AST, which captures the hierarchical relationship between code elements. For instance, in the statement `x = 2 + 3;`, the AST would depict the assignment of the sum of `2` and `3` to the variable `x`.

- Error Recovery: The parser also handles error recovery, attempting to resume parsing after encountering errors to catch as many issues as possible within a single compilation pass.

3. Semantic Analysis: Enforcing Language Rules
Semantic analysis follows syntax analysis and focuses on the meaning and context of the code. It enforces language-specific rules and ensures that the code makes sense from a semantic perspective. Key responsibilities of semantic analysis include:

- Type Checking: The frontend verifies that expressions and assignments are type-safe, ensuring that, for example, you don't try to assign a string to an integer variable.

- Scope Resolution: It tracks variable scopes, ensuring that variables are declared before use and that they are accessible in the correct scope.

- Function Overloading: Some languages allow function overloading, where multiple functions can have the same name but different parameter lists. Semantic analysis resolves which function to call based on the provided arguments.

- Error Detection: Semantic analysis catches a wide range of errors that aren't apparent from the syntax alone. This includes detecting undefined variables, mismatched function arguments, and incompatible types.

- Annotation: During semantic analysis, the frontend may annotate the AST with additional information, such as data types or memory allocation requirements. This information is crucial for later code generation.

Conclusion: The Foundation of Reliable Compilation

The frontend of a compiler, with its responsibilities spanning lexical analysis, syntax analysis, and semantic analysis, is the critical foundation upon which the entire compilation process rests. Its role is akin to that of a skilled artisan, shaping and polishing the raw materials of source code into a structured and meaningful form. A robust frontend ensures that the code is not only syntactically correct but also semantically sound, paving the way for efficient and reliable code generation by the backend. Understanding these frontend responsibilities is key to appreciating the intricacies of compiler construction and the artistry behind transforming human-readable code into machine-executable instructions.

III. Backend Responsibilities
Crafting Machine Code from Abstractions
While the frontend of a compiler interprets, validates, and structures the high-level source code, it's the backend that performs the alchemy, turning these abstract high-level abstractions into tangible machine code ready for execution. The backend is the magician of the compilation process, responsible for tasks ranging from generating intermediate representations (IR) to applying optimizations and finally producing efficient machine code. In this section, we'll delve into the intricacies of the backend, exploring its essential responsibilities, which encompass IR generation, optimization, and code generation.

1. Intermediate Representation (IR) Generation: Bridging the Gap
The first step in the backend's journey is generating an intermediate representation (IR) of the code. The IR serves as a bridge between the high-level source code and the low-level machine code, simplifying subsequent optimization and code generation phases. Key aspects of IR generation include:

- Simplification: The frontend's abstract syntax tree (AST) or similar structure is transformed into a more straightforward representation that is closer to the target machine code but retains enough high-level information for optimization.

- Addressing: During IR generation, the compiler handles memory addressing, including determining stack offsets, heap allocations, and variable storage locations.

- Type Annotations: The IR often includes type information, associating data types with variables, constants, and expressions. This information is crucial for type checking and type-related optimizations.

2. Optimization: Enhancing Efficiency and Performance
After generating the IR, the backend embarks on the optimization phase, where it seeks to improve the efficiency and performance of the generated code. Optimization is a complex and multifaceted task, encompassing a variety of techniques and strategies:

- Constant Folding: Constants within expressions are evaluated at compile-time, reducing runtime overhead.

- Common Subexpression Elimination: Identical subexpressions are computed only once and reused, reducing redundant calculations.

- Dead Code Elimination: Unreachable or redundant code is removed, improving code clarity and execution speed.

- Loop Optimization: The backend analyzes and transforms loops to make them more efficient, employing techniques like loop unrolling, loop fusion, and loop-invariant code motion.

- Register Allocation: The compiler assigns registers to hold intermediate values and variables, aiming to minimize memory access and maximize execution speed.

- Inlining: Small functions or code fragments are inlined directly into the calling code, reducing the overhead of function calls.

- Data Flow Analysis: Sophisticated analyses like reaching definitions and live variable analysis are employed to understand the flow of data in the program, enabling further optimizations.

3. Code Generation: Crafting Machine Code
Code generation is the culmination of the backend's efforts, where it transforms the optimized IR into machine code specific to the target architecture. This phase involves mapping high-level constructs to low-level machine instructions:

- Instruction Selection: The compiler selects appropriate machine instructions to implement high-level operations, taking into account the target architecture's instruction set.

- Register Allocation: Register allocation is revisited, this time considering the specific hardware registers available on the target architecture.

- Instruction Scheduling: For processors with multiple execution units, the backend determines the order in which instructions are executed to maximize parallelism and minimize stalls.

- Memory Management: The backend handles memory allocation and management, including managing stack frames for function calls and allocating memory for dynamically created objects.

- Relocation and Linking: In the case of multiple source files or modules, the backend performs relocation and linking to combine these separate pieces into a single executable or library.

Conclusion: Transforming Abstractions into Action
The backend of a compiler is where the true magic of compilation happens, as it bridges the gap between the high-level abstractions of source code and the concrete reality of machine code. It crafts efficient and performant code through a meticulous process of IR generation, optimization, and code generation. This symphony of tasks, each harmonizing with the others, results in the translation of human-readable code into machine-executable instructions, ready to bring software to life. Understanding the intricacies of backend responsibilities is key to appreciating the power and sophistication of compilers in the modern software development landscape.

IV. Separation of Concerns in Compiler Design
A Symphony of Modular Expertise
In the intricate symphony of compiler design, the principle of separation of concerns takes center stage. This architectural paradigm recognizes that a compiler's complexity can be tamed and its development streamlined by dividing it into distinct, well-defined components, each responsible for a specific aspect of the compilation process. This section delves into the importance of separating concerns in compiler design and explores the pivotal roles played by these modular components, specifically focusing on the frontend and backend.

The Art of Separation

Compiler design is a multifaceted discipline that encompasses lexical analysis, syntax analysis, semantic analysis, optimization, and code generation, among other responsibilities. Attempting to address all these concerns within a monolithic structure would quickly lead to an unwieldy and error-prone system. Instead, compiler designers employ a modular approach that separates these concerns into distinct components, each with a clear and well-defined role.

Frontend: Bridging Syntax and Semantics
The frontend of a compiler is responsible for interpreting and structuring the programmer's high-level source code. Its primary concerns include:

- Lexical Analysis: Tokenizing the source code and recognizing the lexemes within it.

- Syntax Analysis (Parsing): Verifying that the code adheres to the language's syntax rules and constructing a structured representation (e.g., an abstract syntax tree) of the code.

- Semantic Analysis: Ensuring that the code makes sense from a semantic perspective, performing type checking, scope resolution, and error detection.

- Intermediate Representation (IR) Generation: Creating an IR that serves as a bridge between the high-level code and the machine code, simplifying optimization and code generation.

The separation of concerns in the frontend allows each aspect to be tackled independently, fostering code maintainability and easing the addition of support for new languages or language features. It also enables frontend components to be reused across different compilers or tools.

Backend: Transforming Abstractions into Reality
In contrast, the backend of a compiler focuses on generating efficient machine code from the high-level abstractions provided by the frontend. Its primary concerns encompass:

- Intermediate Representation (IR) Optimization: Enhancing the efficiency and performance of the generated code through various optimization techniques.

- Code Generation: Translating the optimized IR into machine code or assembly language specific to the target architecture.

- Register Allocation: Assigning registers to hold intermediate values and variables, aiming to minimize memory access and maximize execution speed.

- Instruction Scheduling: Determining the order in which instructions are executed to maximize parallelism and minimize stalls, crucial for processors with multiple execution units.

- Memory Management: Handling memory allocation and management, including stack frame management for function calls and dynamic memory allocation.

The backend's separation of concerns allows it to target different hardware architectures without needing significant changes to the frontend. It also enables the backend to apply architecture-specific optimizations, enhancing the generated code's performance.

Benefits of Separation of Concerns
The separation of concerns in compiler design yields several advantages:

1. Modularity: Each component focuses on a specific aspect of compilation, simplifying development and maintenance.

2. Reusability: Components can be reused in different compilers or tools, accelerating development and reducing redundancy.

3. Target Independence: Frontends can remain largely independent of the target architecture, facilitating cross-platform development.

4. Optimization Flexibility: The backend can apply architecture-specific optimizations while preserving the frontend's language-agnostic nature.

5. Parallel Development: Teams can work on frontend and backend components in parallel, speeding up the compiler's development cycle.

6. Ease of Extensibility: Support for new languages or language features can be added more easily by modifying or adding frontend components.

Conclusion: Harmonious Compilation
In the world of compiler design, the separation of concerns is the harmonious arrangement that enables the compilation symphony to be orchestrated with precision and efficiency. Each component, whether in the frontend or backend, has a well-defined role, contributing to the modular architecture that makes compilers versatile, maintainable, and adaptable. This separation empowers compiler designers to transform complex high-level source code into efficient machine code, ensuring that software developers can express their ideas in a language of their choice while machines execute those ideas with speed and precision. Understanding the significance of this separation is key

to appreciating the sophistication and power of modern compilers.

V. The Role of Intermediate Representations in Bridging Frontends and Backends

Imagine you're building a bridge that connects two distant lands. The lands represent the frontend and backend of a compiler, separated by the chasm of complexity. To make this connection feasible, you need a solid structure—the bridge—that simplifies the journey while preserving the distinct characteristics of both sides. In the world of compilers, this bridge is the Intermediate Representation (IR).

Understanding Intermediate Representations
An Intermediate Representation (IR) is a structured, machine-independent, and often language-agnostic form of code that serves as a bridge between the frontend and backend of a compiler. It plays a pivotal role in the separation of concerns and facilitates the modular design of compilers. The IR is a medium through which high-level programming concepts can be translated into low-level machine instructions efficiently and accurately. Let's explore the multifaceted role of IRs in bridging the gap between frontend and backend components:

1. Abstraction Preservation:
One of the primary functions of an IR is to preserve the high-level abstractions present in the source code while simplifying the code's structure for optimization and code generation. It strikes a delicate balance between abstractness and concreteness. The IR retains enough high-level information to understand the programmer's intentions while allowing for efficient analysis and transformation.

2. Language Agnosticism:

An ideal IR is language-agnostic, meaning it does not favor any particular programming language. It abstracts away language-specific nuances, enabling the backend to cater to multiple source languages. This versatility is particularly valuable when a compiler supports various programming languages or when developers want to extend a compiler's language support.

3. Facilitating Optimization:
IRs serve as a fertile ground for optimization. Frontend components, which are often language-specific, may not be optimized to the same extent as the backend. The IR acts as an intermediate layer where high-level abstractions can be optimized using language-agnostic techniques. These optimizations include constant folding, common subexpression elimination, and dead code removal, among others.

4. Simplifying Code Generation:
Translating high-level code into machine code can be a daunting task. The IR abstracts away many intricacies of the target machine, making code generation more manageable. It provides a level of indirection between the frontend and backend, allowing the backend to focus on the target machine's specific details.

5. Target Architecture Neutrality:
A well-designed IR should be neutral with respect to the target architecture. This neutrality enables the same frontend to generate code for different machine architectures by coupling it with distinct backends. For example, a C compiler frontend can use the same IR for generating code on both x86 and ARM processors.

6. Cross-Component Communication:
The IR acts as a communication channel between the frontend and backend components. It allows the frontend to hand over a structured representation of the code to

the backend, where it can undergo optimization and code generation without the need for the frontend's active involvement.

7. Debugging and Profiling:
IRs are also invaluable for debugging and profiling tools. They provide an intermediate point where developers can inspect and analyze code during compilation. This helps in identifying optimization opportunities, diagnosing errors, and improving overall code quality.

Conclusion: The Bridge of Translation
In the symphony of compiler design, Intermediate Representations are the bridges that span the chasm between the frontend's high-level abstractions and the backend's low-level machine code. They encapsulate the essence of a program's logic while simplifying the complexities of translation and optimization. These bridges enable compilers to be versatile, maintainable, and extendable, making it possible for programmers to express their ideas in their preferred high-level language while machines execute those ideas efficiently. The role of IRs in compiler design is a testament to the elegance and power of modular separation in the creation of sophisticated software tools.

Chapter 10: Compiler Tools and Toolchains

I. Introduction to Compiler Construction Tools

Crafting the Compiler's Arsenal
Compiler construction is a monumental task, akin to building a grand cathedral of code. To undertake such a venture, developers rely on a sophisticated arsenal of tools that aid in every facet of compiler design, from parsing source code to generating efficient machine instructions. In this chapter, we embark on a journey to explore the vast landscape of compiler construction tools, examining their vital roles, classifications, and how they collectively orchestrate the compilation process.

The Multifaceted Nature of Compiler Tools
Compiler construction is not a solitary endeavor but rather a collaborative effort that involves a myriad of tools, each contributing a unique set of capabilities. These tools are instrumental in taming the complexity of the compilation process and ensuring that compilers can efficiently translate high-level source code into machine-executable instructions.

1. Lexical and Syntax Analysis Tools:
At the frontend of a compiler, lexical analysis tools such as Flex (a successor to Lex) and syntax analysis tools like Bison (or Yacc) play pivotal roles. Lexical analyzers break down the source code into tokens, while syntax analyzers validate the code's structure against a grammar and construct abstract syntax trees (ASTs). These tools automate the generation of code for these critical phases, saving compiler developers from having to craft them by hand.

2. Semantic Analysis and Intermediate Code Generation Tools:

Tools like ANTLR (ANother Tool for Language Recognition) and LLVM (Low-Level Virtual Machine) are indispensable for implementing semantic analysis and generating intermediate representations (IRs). ANTLR simplifies the creation of parsers and provides the foundation for building custom frontends. LLVM, on the other hand, offers a comprehensive infrastructure for generating and optimizing IRs, serving as a bridge between frontend and backend components.

3. Code Generation Tools:
Code generation for various target architectures is a complex task. Compilers often employ code generation tools like GCC (GNU Compiler Collection) and Microsoft Visual C++ to emit efficient machine code for different processors. These tools encapsulate the intricacies of instruction selection, register allocation, and instruction scheduling, allowing compiler developers to focus on optimizing code for specific target architectures.

4. Optimization Tools:
The optimization phase is where compilers strive to make generated code more efficient. Compiler optimization tools, such as LLVM's optimization passes and GCC's optimization framework, provide a rich set of optimization techniques. These tools enable compiler writers to apply a wide range of optimizations, from basic constant folding to sophisticated loop transformations.

5. Debugging and Profiling Tools:
Debugging and profiling are integral to compiler development. Tools like GDB (GNU Debugger) and Valgrind help identify and rectify errors in the compiler itself and provide a means to analyze the behavior of generated code. Profiling tools offer insights into the runtime performance of compiled programs, aiding in further optimization.

6. Build Systems and Automation Tools:
Build systems like Make and CMake simplify the process of compiling large-scale software projects, including compilers. These tools manage dependencies, automate the build process, and facilitate project configuration. For compiler development, they ensure that the myriad components and libraries that comprise a compiler are assembled correctly.

7. Version Control Systems:
Version control systems like Git and Subversion are indispensable for tracking changes, managing collaborative development, and ensuring the integrity of compiler source code. They enable distributed development teams to work seamlessly on compiler projects.

Conclusion: Crafting the Compiler's Symphony
Compiler construction tools are the virtuoso musicians in the symphony of compiler development. They bring precision, efficiency, and automation to the intricate process of transforming high-level code into machine-executable instructions. By harnessing these tools, compiler developers craft the instruments that empower programmers to express their ideas in their preferred languages, all while ensuring that machines can execute those ideas with speed and accuracy. Understanding the diverse roles and capabilities of these tools is essential to appreciating the artistry and complexity of compiler construction.

II. Compiler Toolchains and Their Components
The Symphony of Compilation
Compiler development is not merely about crafting a single monolithic tool. Instead, it's about assembling a symphony of individual instruments, each with its own role and expertise. This harmonious ensemble of tools is what we refer to as a "compiler toolchain." In this

section, we delve into the intricacies of compiler toolchains, dissecting their components and exploring how they collaboratively produce the beautiful music of code compilation.

The Compiler Toolchain: An Orchestra of Tools

Imagine an orchestra preparing for a grand performance. In this analogy, the compiler toolchain is the orchestra, and each component is a skilled musician playing a unique instrument. Together, they create a harmonious composition from the raw source code.

1. Preprocessor: The Tuning Fork

The preprocessor is the tuning fork of the orchestra, setting the tone for the compilation process. It handles directives like `#include` and `#define`, performing textual transformations on the source code before it undergoes compilation. The output of the preprocessor is often referred to as "preprocessed code."

2. Compiler: The Soloists

The compiler is the soloist, the central performer in the ensemble. It takes the preprocessed code and translates it into assembly code or intermediate representations (IRs). The compiler is responsible for lexing, parsing, semantic analysis, optimization, and code generation. It creates the heart of the machine-executable program.

3. Assembler: The Conductor

The assembler is the conductor of the orchestra, orchestrating the assembly of the machine code from the assembly code produced by the compiler. It translates the symbolic assembly code into binary machine code, resolving memory addresses and managing relocation.

4. Linker: The Ensemble Coordinator

In an orchestra, various sections (strings, brass, woodwinds) must coordinate their efforts. Similarly, in software development, separate source files and libraries need coordination. The linker is the ensemble coordinator, bringing together different pieces of compiled code, resolving dependencies, and producing a single executable program. It handles functions like resolving external references, merging object files, and allocating memory.

5. Libraries: The Supporting Cast
Libraries are like the supporting cast, providing essential functions and routines that can be reused across different programs. Standard libraries (e.g., C Standard Library) offer a plethora of functions to assist programmers in their tasks. Developers can also create their own libraries to encapsulate commonly used code.

6. Build Tools: The Stage Managers
Build tools, such as Make, CMake, and Gradle, act as stage managers, overseeing the entire production. They automate the compilation process, tracking dependencies, ensuring that only the necessary files are recompiled, and coordinating the execution of the entire toolchain. Build tools streamline the development process, especially for large-scale projects.

7. Debugger: The Sound Engineer
When the orchestra encounters issues during a performance, a sound engineer helps identify and fix problems. Similarly, a debugger is a sound engineer for software development. It allows developers to inspect and manipulate the program's execution, set breakpoints, and diagnose issues, ensuring that the code performs as expected.

8. Profilers: The Critics and Audience
Profiling tools are like critics and audience members who assess the performance. They monitor the program's execution, collect data on resource usage (CPU,

memory, I/O), and provide insights into performance bottlenecks. Profilers help developers fine-tune their code for optimal execution.

Conclusion: The Beautiful Composition
In the world of compiler development, the compiler toolchain is a symphony of meticulously crafted components. Each tool plays a crucial role, contributing its expertise to the production of efficient and reliable software. Like the instruments in an orchestra, these components must harmonize seamlessly to create the beautiful composition of compiled code. Understanding their roles and interactions is essential for both compiler developers and software engineers who rely on the compiler's performance and correctness to bring their ideas to life.

III. Building and Configuring a Complete Compiler Toolchain

Crafting Your Symphony
Creating a complete compiler toolchain is akin to assembling a symphony orchestra, where each instrument must be carefully selected, tuned, and coordinated to produce a harmonious performance. In this section, we embark on a journey to explore the process of building and configuring a complete compiler toolchain, from selecting the components to fine-tuning their interactions.

The Essence of a Complete Toolchain
A complete compiler toolchain is a set of software tools that collectively enable the transformation of source code into executable programs. To build a toolchain from scratch, you need to carefully select and configure each component, ensuring that they work seamlessly together. Here's how you can compose your symphony:

1. Selecting the Compiler: Your Principal Soloist

The heart of any compiler toolchain is the compiler itself. Depending on your project requirements and target languages, you might choose a compiler like GCC (GNU Compiler Collection) for C/C++ or Clang for a more modular and modern alternative. Select a compiler that supports your target architecture and offers the features you need.

2. Choosing the Right Assembler: Conductor of the Orchestra

The assembler is the conductor that translates assembly code into machine code. For compatibility with your chosen compiler, select an assembler that aligns with your project's architecture and operating system. Common choices include GAS (GNU Assembler) and NASM (Netwide Assembler).

3. Picking the Linker: Coordinator of Sections

The linker's role is to coordinate the various sections of your program, including object files and libraries. The GNU linker, LD, is a widely used choice, but you can also consider other linkers like LLVM's LLD. Ensure that the linker supports the object file format generated by your assembler and compiler.

4. Integrating Libraries: The Supporting Ensemble

Libraries are vital for reusing code and avoiding unnecessary redundancy. The C Standard Library (libc) is a fundamental library for C programs. Other language-specific libraries and third-party libraries are available for additional functionality. Ensure that these libraries are compatible with your chosen compiler and linker.

5. Utilizing Build Tools: The Stage Managers

To automate the compilation process and manage dependencies, choose a build tool like Make, CMake, or Gradle. These tools simplify the orchestration of your compiler toolchain. Configure them to build your project, specifying compiler options, linker flags, and library dependencies.

6. Debugging and Profiling: The Sound Engineers and Critics

For debugging, employ a debugger like GDB (GNU Debugger) or LLDB (Low-Level Debugger) that integrates seamlessly with your chosen compiler. Profiling tools, such as perf and Valgrind, help identify performance bottlenecks and resource utilization.

7. Cross-Compilers: Expanding Your Repertoire

If your project involves targeting different architectures or platforms, consider cross-compilers. These compilers generate code for a target architecture different from the host system. Cross-compilers are essential for embedded systems and cross-platform development.

8. Configuration and Environment Setup: Tuning the Instruments

Configure environment variables and paths to ensure that each component of your toolchain is discoverable and correctly invoked. Set compiler options, optimization levels, and debugging symbols as needed for your project.

9. Testing and Validation: The Dress Rehearsal

Before unleashing your symphony of code into the world, thoroughly test and validate your toolchain. Ensure that it can compile, link, and execute your programs correctly. Write comprehensive test suites to assess its functionality and reliability.

10. Documentation and Maintenance: Preserving the Score

Document your toolchain's configuration, dependencies, and any customizations. Maintain version control for all components to track changes and facilitate collaboration.

Regularly update and fine-tune your toolchain to adapt to evolving project requirements.

Conclusion: Crafting Your Compiler Masterpiece
Building and configuring a complete compiler toolchain is a complex but rewarding endeavor. Just like a conductor crafting a symphony, you carefully select, tune, and coordinate each component to create a harmonious ensemble. Your toolchain empowers you to transform source code into performant and reliable executable programs, allowing your software projects to shine as musical masterpieces in the world of computing. Understanding the nuances of each component and their interactions is essential for producing exceptional software and advancing your skills in the art of compiler development.

IV. Compiler Optimization Levels
Fine-Tuning Your Code's Performance
Optimizing software is akin to crafting a piece of fine art. Compiler optimization levels serve as your palette, allowing you to apply strokes of optimization techniques to your code. In this section, we delve into the intricacies of compiler optimization levels, exploring how they can dramatically impact your code's performance and behavior.

Understanding Compiler Optimization
Compiler optimization is the art of transforming source code to make it execute more efficiently while preserving its correctness. Optimization aims to reduce execution time, improve code size, and minimize resource usage. However, it's important to note that optimizations are not without trade-offs, and they can sometimes introduce subtle bugs or undesired side effects.

Compiler Optimization Levels

Compiler optimization levels are a set of predefined configurations that instruct the compiler on the degree of optimization to apply when compiling your code. These levels provide a balance between the effort invested in optimization and the resulting performance gains. Let's explore the common optimization levels offered by most compilers:

1. No Optimization (O0): At this level, the compiler performs no optimization. Your code is compiled as-is, making it easier to debug and understand but potentially less efficient in terms of execution speed and memory usage. It's suitable for development and debugging phases.

2. Minimal Optimization (O1 or -O1): Minimal optimization focuses on improving code execution speed while keeping the generated code relatively simple. It includes optimizations like constant propagation and dead code elimination. This level aims to provide a noticeable performance boost without sacrificing code readability or debuggability.

3. Moderate Optimization (O2 or -O2): Moderate optimization increases the level of effort the compiler puts into making your code faster. It includes more aggressive optimizations like loop unrolling, function inlining, and common subexpression elimination. While it can significantly enhance performance, it may also lead to larger executable sizes and slightly longer compilation times.

4. High Optimization (O3 or -O3): High optimization is where the compiler pulls out its most potent tricks. It applies advanced and potentially time-consuming optimizations, such as aggressive loop optimizations, instruction scheduling, and vectorization. Code generated at this level can be significantly faster, but

compilation times may increase, and the resulting binary may be larger.

5. Maximum Optimization (Ofast or -Ofast): This level aims for maximum performance and might sacrifice some standard compliance and safety checks. It can enable aggressive optimizations like fast-math flags, which allow optimizations that could result in small deviations in floating-point calculations. While it can yield impressive speed improvements, it should be used with caution, especially in safety-critical or standards-compliant code.

6. Size Optimization (Os or -Os): Size optimization focuses on minimizing the generated binary's size rather than execution speed. It applies optimizations that reduce code size, like function inlining and dead code elimination. This level is suitable for embedded systems or situations where code size is a critical factor.

7. Custom Optimization (Custom Flags): Some compilers allow you to fine-tune optimization by specifying custom flags. This approach offers maximum control but requires a deep understanding of optimization techniques and their potential effects on your code.

Choosing the Right Optimization Level
Selecting the appropriate optimization level depends on your project's requirements and constraints. Consider the following factors:

- Performance goals: If you need the highest possible execution speed, opt for higher optimization levels like O3 or Ofast.
- Debugging and development: During development and debugging, lower optimization levels (O0 or O1) are preferred to aid in code inspection and debugging.

- Code size: When targeting resource-constrained environments, size optimization (Os) may be necessary.
- Safety and compliance: In safety-critical or standards-compliant applications, avoid potentially risky optimizations like Ofast.

It's essential to profile and benchmark your code with different optimization levels to determine which one strikes the best balance between performance and other requirements. Additionally, remember that compiler optimizations can sometimes interact with specific code patterns in unexpected ways, so thorough testing is crucial to ensure correctness.

Conclusion: Mastering the Art of Optimization
Compiler optimization levels provide a powerful toolset for enhancing your code's performance and resource utilization. Just as a painter selects different brushes and colors to create a masterpiece, you can leverage optimization levels to fine-tune your code's execution characteristics. Whether your goal is blazing-fast execution, minimal memory usage, or standards compliance, understanding and mastering optimization levels is an essential skill for every compiler developer and software engineer.

V. Cross-Compilation and Portability Issues
Navigating the Multiverse of Platforms
In the realm of compiler tools and toolchains, cross-compilation emerges as a pivotal concept. It's a technique that enables the creation of software on one platform, known as the host, for execution on another, known as the target. This process isn't merely a technicality; it's a critical skill in addressing portability issues and reaching a broader audience. In this section, we embark on a journey to explore the intricacies of cross-compilation and the challenges it presents in the quest for platform independence.

The Need for Cross-Compilation
Imagine a scenario where you're developing software for a diverse ecosystem of devices and architectures. Some of these devices may use specialized processors, others could run different operating systems, and a few might even reside in remote embedded systems. Compiling your software natively on each target platform would be impractical, time-consuming, and error-prone. This is where cross-compilation steps in to save the day.

The Host-Target Relationship
In cross-compilation, two platforms come into play: the host and the target. Here's what these terms mean:

1. Host Platform: The host is the system where you run the compiler and other development tools. This is your development machine, and it generates machine code for the target platform.

2. Target Platform: The target is the system where the compiled code will ultimately execute. It could be a different architecture, operating system, or even an embedded system with limited resources.

Challenges in Cross-Compilation
Cross-compilation isn't without its challenges. Several factors make it a complex endeavor:

1. Differences in Architecture: The host and target platforms may have distinct CPU architectures, such as x86, ARM, MIPS, or PowerPC. Generating code for a different architecture requires adjusting the compiler and assembler settings.

2. Diverse Operating Systems: The host and target might run different operating systems, each with its own system calls, libraries, and file systems. Cross-

compilation must address these discrepancies to ensure the generated code functions correctly.

3. Library and Header Files: Compilers rely on libraries and header files for various platform-specific functionalities. Cross-compilation necessitates the availability of compatible libraries and headers for the target platform.

4. Endianness: Some architectures have different byte orders (endianness), which affects how data is stored and processed. Cross-compilation must consider endianness differences.

5. Resource Constraints: Embedded systems or devices with limited resources pose unique challenges. Cross-compilation must generate efficient code and adapt to resource constraints.

Cross-Compilation Workflow
To embark on a cross-compilation journey, you'll follow a workflow that ensures the successful generation of code for the target platform:

1. Toolchain Selection: Choose a cross-compiler toolchain designed for your target platform. Toolchains often include a cross-compiler, linker, and libraries tailored to the target architecture and operating system.

2. Configuration: Configure the cross-compiler with information about the target platform, including architecture, operating system, and any platform-specific settings.

3. Cross-Compilation: Write or adapt your source code to be portable and platform-independent. Then, compile it using the cross-compiler, which generates binary code for the target platform.

4. Testing and Debugging: Testing on the target platform is crucial to ensure correct functionality. Debugging tools for cross-compiled code may differ from those used on the host platform.

5. Deployment: Deploy the compiled code to the target platform, taking into account any platform-specific requirements for installation and execution.

Addressing Portability Issues
Cross-compilation is a powerful technique for addressing portability issues in software development. It enables developers to target a wide range of platforms without the need for separate development environments. However, achieving true platform independence requires careful consideration of the following aspects:

1. Platform-Agnostic Code: Write code that is as platform-agnostic as possible. Avoid platform-specific dependencies and use portable libraries and APIs whenever feasible.

2. Conditional Compilation: Use conditional compilation directives to include or exclude platform-specific code sections based on predefined macros and compiler flags.

3. Abstraction Layers: Implement abstraction layers and interfaces that encapsulate platform-specific functionality. This allows you to provide different implementations for different platforms.

4. Testing Across Platforms: Rigorously test your software on all target platforms to identify and address portability issues.

Conclusion: Bridging the Platform Divide

Cross-compilation is a bridge that connects the multiverse of computing platforms, enabling software to transcend boundaries and run seamlessly on diverse devices and architectures. While it presents challenges, mastering cross-compilation is an essential skill for software developers who aim to reach a broader audience and ensure their code's portability. It's a testament to the ever-evolving landscape of technology, where adaptability and versatility are the keys to success in the ever-expanding universe of computing.

Chapter 11: Recent Advances and Future Trends

I. Recent Developments in Compiler Technology
Pioneering the Path Forward
Compiler technology, the silent enabler of modern computing, continually evolves to keep pace with the ever-advancing world of software and hardware. In this section, we embark on a journey through recent developments in compiler technology, exploring the innovative techniques and paradigms that are shaping the future of software development.

1. Just-In-Time (JIT) Compilation: Real-Time Performance
Just-In-Time (JIT) compilation, a technique initially popularized by Java and later embraced by other languages like JavaScript and C#, has gained significant traction. JIT compilers translate high-level code into machine code at runtime, enabling optimizations tailored to the executing environment. Recent advancements in JIT compilation include profile-guided optimizations, speculative optimizations, and adaptive compilation, which adapt code generation based on runtime feedback. This dynamic approach enhances performance, making JIT compilation an invaluable tool for applications like web browsers, virtual machines, and game engines.

2. Machine Learning-Driven Optimizations: Intelligent Code Improvement
Machine learning has entered the realm of compiler technology, promising smarter and more adaptive code optimizations. By training models on vast datasets of code and performance profiles, compilers can now make informed decisions about which optimizations to apply and when. These "learned" optimizations can significantly boost execution speed while reducing the

need for human intervention. Machine learning-driven optimizations are particularly promising for generating efficient code for neural networks and other AI workloads.

3. Polyhedral Compilation: Bridging the Gap for Parallelism

Polyhedral compilation, a complex mathematical framework, is revolutionizing how compilers handle parallelism and optimization in loop-intensive code. Recent developments in this field have led to more accessible tools and techniques for identifying and exploiting parallelism in programs. Polyhedral compilers can automatically transform loops to take full advantage of multi-core processors and accelerators, making them indispensable for scientific computing, data analytics, and simulations.

4. WebAssembly (Wasm): A Universal Execution Target

WebAssembly (Wasm) has emerged as a universal binary format for web applications, enabling code to run efficiently in web browsers across different platforms. Wasm supports multiple programming languages and serves as a compilation target for both ahead-of-time (AOT) and just-in-time (JIT) compilers. Recent developments in Wasm focus on improving runtime performance, security, and compatibility, making it a pivotal technology for cross-platform web applications.

5. Quantum Compilation: Preparing for the Quantum Era

As quantum computing advances, compilers face the unique challenge of preparing code for quantum processors. Quantum compilation involves translating quantum algorithms written in high-level languages into instructions that quantum hardware can execute. Recent work in this field has produced quantum circuit optimization techniques, quantum error correction support, and quantum assembly languages. Quantum compilation is laying the groundwork for a future where quantum computing is seamlessly integrated into classical software.

6. Domain-Specific Language (DSL) Compilers: Tailoring for Efficiency

Domain-specific languages (DSLs) are gaining popularity due to their ability to express complex domain-specific tasks concisely. Compiler technology plays a pivotal role in optimizing DSL code for efficiency. Recent advancements in DSL compilers include automatic parallelization, vectorization, and hardware acceleration. These developments empower developers to harness the full potential of DSLs without sacrificing performance.

7. Open-Source Compiler Ecosystems: Collaborative Innovation

The open-source compiler ecosystem, with projects like LLVM and GCC at its core, continues to thrive. Recent contributions from the open-source community have led to improvements in performance, support for new programming languages, and enhanced compiler extensions. These ecosystems foster collaborative innovation, ensuring that compiler technology remains at the forefront of software development.

Conclusion: The Compiler Renaissance

The world of compilers is undergoing a renaissance, driven by the demands of modern computing. Recent advancements in compiler technology are breaking new ground, enabling developers to create more efficient, secure, and adaptable software. As we peer into the future, we can anticipate even more exciting developments, with compilers at the vanguard of innovation in the ever-evolving landscape of computing. The path forward is illuminated by the promise of smarter, more efficient, and more accessible software development.

II. Just-in-Time Compilation and Dynamic Optimization

Code That Adapts on the Fly

In the fast-paced world of software development, performance is often the key differentiator between success and obscurity. Just-in-time compilation (JIT) and dynamic optimization have emerged as dynamic duos, poised to meet the ever-growing demands for real-time performance and adaptability. This section explores how JIT compilation and dynamic optimization work together to create code that evolves and adapts on the fly.

The JIT Compilation Paradigm

JIT compilation represents a departure from the traditional static compilation model. Instead of translating source code into machine code ahead of time, a JIT compiler defers compilation until runtime. This dynamic approach opens a world of possibilities for optimization and adaptability:

1. Late-Binding: JIT compilers wait until the last possible moment, just before execution, to generate machine code. This allows them to make decisions based on runtime information, such as the specific hardware architecture and usage patterns.

2. Profile-Guided Optimization (PGO): JIT compilers can collect performance data during program execution and use this information to make informed optimization decisions. For example, if a certain code path is frequently executed, the JIT compiler can apply aggressive optimizations to that path.

3. Adaptive Compilation: JIT compilers can switch between different optimization levels or strategies

depending on the context. For example, they might employ less aggressive optimizations for quick startup times and ramp up to more aggressive optimizations as the program continues running.

4. Platform Independence: JIT compilation can bridge the gap between different hardware architectures. By generating machine code tailored to the host machine, JIT compilers enable the same high-level code to run efficiently on a variety of platforms.

Dynamic Optimization Techniques
Dynamic optimization complements JIT compilation by continuously refining code based on runtime behavior. These techniques are the engine that drives the adaptability of JIT-compiled code:

1. Inlining: Dynamic inlining involves the selective inlining of functions or methods based on their usage patterns. Frequently called functions can be inlined to eliminate the overhead of function calls, while less frequently called ones can be left as separate functions to save memory.

2. Dead Code Elimination: As a program runs, dynamic optimization can identify and eliminate sections of code that are never executed. This not only reduces memory footprint but also speeds up execution by removing unnecessary branches.

3. Speculative Optimization: Dynamic optimization allows compilers to speculate on future execution paths based on observed patterns. For example, if a loop typically iterates a certain number of times, the compiler can optimize for that case, even before it occurs.

4. Re-optimization: Dynamic optimization isn't a one-time affair. JIT compilers can continuously monitor program

behavior and re-optimize code as it evolves. This ensures that the code remains efficient even as the workload changes.

Use Cases and Benefits
JIT compilation and dynamic optimization have found their place in various domains:

1. Web Browsers: JIT compilation powers modern JavaScript engines, enabling fast execution of web applications. Browsers use dynamic optimization to adapt to changing user interactions and webpage content.

2. Virtual Machines: Virtual machines for languages like Java and Python employ JIT compilers to execute bytecode efficiently. Dynamic optimization helps these languages achieve near-native performance.

3. Gaming: Game engines utilize JIT compilation to deliver high-performance graphics and physics simulations. Dynamic optimization ensures smooth gameplay even on diverse hardware.

4. Scientific Computing: In scientific applications, JIT compilation can adapt to varying input data sizes and computational workloads, delivering optimized performance for simulations and data analysis.

5. Mobile Apps: JIT compilation is a common feature in mobile app development. It allows apps to start quickly while optimizing critical code paths over time.

Challenges and Considerations
While JIT compilation and dynamic optimization offer impressive benefits, they come with challenges:

1. Overhead: The initial compilation overhead can affect startup times. JIT compilers must strike a balance between fast startup and long-term performance gains.

2. Security: JIT compilers need to be vigilant about security. Compromised code can have devastating consequences, so JIT compilers must employ strict security checks.

3. Warm-Up Period: It takes time for JIT-compiled code to reach its peak performance. During the "warm-up" period, code may not be as optimized as it could be.

4. Resource Usage: Dynamic optimization can consume additional CPU and memory resources. JIT compilers must manage these resources efficiently.

Conclusion: The Shape-Shifting Code of Tomorrow
Just-in-time compilation and dynamic optimization represent the future of software performance. In a world where adaptability and speed are paramount, JIT-compiled code that evolves and optimizes on the fly is becoming increasingly essential. As these technologies continue to mature, we can expect software to become more efficient, responsive, and capable of meeting the ever-growing demands of modern computing.

III. Parallel and GPU Programming Support
Harnessing the Power of Multicore and Accelerated Computing

In the dynamic landscape of software development, where computational demands continue to surge, the ability to leverage parallelism and harness the potential of Graphics Processing Units (GPUs) has emerged as a game-changer. This section delves into the transformative realm of parallel and GPU programming support in modern compilers, unraveling the techniques and innovations that are reshaping the future of high-performance computing.

The Era of Multicore Processors and GPUs

The relentless pursuit of performance gains in computing has given rise to multicore processors and GPUs as mainstream hardware architectures. Instead of relying solely on increased clock speeds, modern processors now feature multiple cores, allowing for concurrent execution of tasks. GPUs, originally designed for rendering graphics, have evolved into massively parallel processors capable of tackling a wide range of computational workloads.

Compiler Support for Parallelism

Parallel programming is both a challenge and an opportunity. Developers seek ways to exploit parallelism in their applications, but doing so manually can be complex and error-prone. This is where compilers come into play, offering support for parallelism in various forms:

1. Auto-Vectorization: Compilers analyze loops and data dependencies to automatically generate SIMD (Single Instruction, Multiple Data) instructions. This technique, known as auto-vectorization, accelerates numerical computations by exploiting parallelism within the data.

2. Threading Support: Multithreading, a technique where multiple threads run concurrently, is a vital form of parallelism. Compilers provide threading support through libraries like OpenMP and Pthreads, allowing developers to express parallelism in their code and letting the compiler handle thread management.

3. Task-Based Parallelism: Task-based parallelism is a higher-level approach that abstracts the parallel execution of tasks. Compilers offer support for task-

based parallelism, making it easier to express parallelism and take advantage of multicore processors.

4. GPU Acceleration: To tap into the immense computational power of GPUs, compilers enable developers to offload specific code segments to the GPU. This is known as GPU acceleration or GPGPU (General-Purpose GPU) programming. Popular GPU programming languages like CUDA and OpenCL are supported by modern compilers.

GPU Programming Support
Graphics Processing Units, once confined to gaming and graphics rendering, have now become formidable accelerators for a wide range of computational tasks, including scientific simulations, machine learning, and data processing. Compiler support for GPU programming has evolved significantly:

1. CUDA and OpenCL Integration: Compilers support CUDA and OpenCL, enabling developers to write GPU-accelerated code directly in high-level programming languages like C and C++. Compilers assist in generating the necessary GPU-specific code, simplifying the development process.

2. GPU Code Analysis: Compilers perform static code analysis to identify code sections suitable for GPU acceleration. They also generate GPU-specific kernel code, manage data transfers between CPU and GPU memory, and optimize the overall GPU execution.

3. Unified Memory: Modern compilers and GPUs offer unified memory architectures, blurring the distinction between CPU and GPU memory. This simplifies data management and enables seamless data sharing between the CPU and GPU, reducing the complexity of GPU programming.

4. GPU Libraries: Compilers often include GPU-accelerated libraries that provide pre-optimized functions for common tasks, such as linear algebra operations and image processing. These libraries allow developers to harness GPU power without delving into low-level GPU programming.

Benefits and Challenges
Parallel and GPU programming support in compilers offer several benefits:

1. Performance Gains: By harnessing parallelism, applications can achieve significant performance improvements, reducing execution times and enabling the processing of larger datasets.

2. Code Portability: Compiler support for GPU programming abstracts hardware-specific details, making it easier to write code that can run on a variety of GPU architectures.

3. Developer Productivity: Developers can focus on high-level algorithmic design while letting compilers handle the intricacies of parallelism and GPU execution.

However, challenges persist:

1. Scalability: Achieving optimal parallelism and GPU performance requires careful design and tuning. Not all applications can be parallelized effectively.

2. Debugging Complexity: Debugging parallel and GPU code can be challenging due to the non-deterministic nature of parallel execution and limited debugging tools.

3. Learning Curve: Effectively utilizing parallelism and GPUs often requires a learning curve, as developers

must understand the intricacies of parallel programming models and GPU architectures.

Conclusion: Empowering the Era of Parallelism
Parallel and GPU programming support in modern compilers is a testament to the evolving landscape of high-performance computing. As the demand for computational power continues to surge, compilers play a pivotal role in democratizing parallelism and GPU acceleration. The future holds the promise of even more sophisticated compiler techniques, enabling developers to tap into the full potential of multicore processors and GPUs while abstracting the complexity of parallel programming. With these tools at their disposal, developers are poised to unlock new frontiers in computational capabilities and reshape the world of software and science.

IV. Integration with IDEs and Development Environments
The Synergy of Compiler and Code
In the ever-evolving landscape of software development, the synergy between compilers and Integrated Development Environments (IDEs) has ushered in a new era of productivity and code quality. This section explores how compilers have seamlessly integrated with IDEs and development environments, shaping the way developers write, test, and optimize code.

IDEs as the Developer's Workbench
Integrated Development Environments have long been the epicenter of software development. These comprehensive toolsets provide developers with a unified platform for coding, debugging, and project management. The integration of compilers within IDEs has brought a myriad of advantages:

1. Real-time Compilation: IDEs offer real-time compilation feedback, instantly highlighting syntax errors and compilation issues as you type. This immediate feedback loop accelerates development and reduces debugging time.

2. Code Navigation: IDEs seamlessly integrate with compilers to provide advanced code navigation features. Developers can jump to function definitions, find usages, and explore code hierarchies with ease.

3. Intelligent Code Completion: Modern IDEs incorporate intelligent code completion powered by compiler analysis. As you type, the IDE suggests code snippets, method names, and variable types, enhancing code quality and reducing typos.

4. Refactoring Support: Compilers integrated with IDEs enable sophisticated code refactoring capabilities. Developers can safely rename variables, extract methods, and perform other refactorings, with the assurance that the compiler will catch any errors.

5. Debugging Assistance: IDEs offer debugging features that rely on compiler-generated debug information. This includes setting breakpoints, inspecting variables, and stepping through code, all made possible by the tight integration with the compiler.

6. Performance Profiling: Compilers help IDEs provide performance profiling tools. Developers can analyze code execution, memory usage, and CPU performance, allowing for optimization at an early stage.

IDEs of the Future: Intelligent Assistance
The future of IDE-compiler integration is marked by intelligent assistance:

1. Predictive Code Suggestions: IDEs will leverage compiler insights and machine learning to predict the next lines of code you're likely to write, making coding faster and more intuitive.

2. Code Review Automation: IDEs will provide automated code review suggestions based on compiler analysis, helping developers catch potential issues before they reach production.

3. Code Optimization Guidance: Advanced IDEs will offer proactive optimization suggestions, guiding developers on how to write more efficient code based on compiler insights.

4. Error Prevention: IDEs will evolve to prevent common coding mistakes at the source, thanks to compiler-driven insights into best practices and coding standards.

5. Seamless Collaboration: Future IDEs will enable real-time collaboration with colleagues, leveraging compiler knowledge to resolve code conflicts and maintain consistency.

Challenges and Considerations
While the integration of compilers with IDEs offers immense benefits, several challenges must be addressed:

1. Performance: Real-time compilation and analysis can introduce latency in the development process, impacting developer productivity. Optimizing the performance of compiler-IDE interactions is essential.

2. Compatibility: Maintaining compatibility with various compilers, programming languages, and development environments can be complex. IDE developers must ensure seamless integration across diverse toolchains.

3. Learning Curve: Leveraging advanced IDE features requires developers to learn and adapt to new workflows, potentially causing initial productivity dips.

Conclusion: The Evolution of Developer Empowerment
The integration of compilers with IDEs and development environments represents a powerful union that empowers developers to write cleaner, more efficient code with greater ease. As we look to the future, this synergy promises to become even more intelligent and sophisticated, supporting developers in every aspect of their coding journey. The integrated compiler-IDE ecosystem is a testament to the relentless pursuit of efficiency and quality in software development, and it will continue to drive innovation and elevate the art of programming.

V. The Impact of Machine Learning on Compiler Optimization
A Revolution in Code Efficiency
The intersection of machine learning and compiler optimization has given rise to a revolution in the world of code efficiency. This section delves into the profound impact of machine learning on compiler optimization, showcasing how artificial intelligence and neural networks are transforming the way compilers optimize code.

Traditional Compiler Optimization: A Foundation
Compiler optimization has long been a cornerstone of software development. Traditional optimization techniques involve analyzing code to improve execution speed and reduce memory consumption. These optimizations include loop unrolling, constant propagation, and dead code elimination. While these techniques have significantly enhanced code performance over the years, they are often heuristic-

based and lack adaptability to diverse codebases and architectures.

The Machine Learning Paradigm

Machine learning has emerged as a transformative force, capable of learning complex patterns and making data-driven decisions. When applied to compiler optimization, machine learning introduces a new paradigm:

1. Code Analysis: Machine learning models are trained on vast datasets of code snippets and their corresponding performance profiles. These models analyze code structures, data access patterns, and execution paths to identify optimization opportunities.

2. Adaptive Optimization: Unlike static heuristics, machine learning models adapt to the specific characteristics of the code being compiled. They make context-aware decisions to choose the most effective optimizations, considering factors like code size, execution frequency, and memory constraints.

3. Predictive Compilation: Machine learning models can predict the performance impact of different optimizations before applying them. This allows compilers to explore optimization options intelligently and choose the most beneficial ones, reducing the risk of performance regressions.

4. Cross-Platform Optimization: Machine learning-driven compilers can optimize code for various target architectures, dynamically adapting to the underlying hardware. This cross-platform adaptability is crucial in the era of diverse computing platforms.

Machine Learning Techniques in Compiler Optimization

Several machine learning techniques are applied in compiler optimization:

1. Supervised Learning: Supervised learning models are trained on labeled datasets, where each code snippet is associated with its optimized version. These models can predict optimizations based on code features and context.

2. Reinforcement Learning: Reinforcement learning agents interact with a compiler environment, taking actions (applying optimizations) to maximize a reward signal (improved performance). Over time, these agents learn to make optimal decisions.

3. Neural Networks: Deep neural networks, such as convolutional neural networks (CNNs) and recurrent neural networks (RNNs), are used to extract patterns and features from code, enabling advanced code analysis and optimization decisions.

4. Genetic Algorithms: Genetic algorithms mimic the process of natural selection to evolve code optimizations. They generate and test various optimization strategies, gradually refining them to achieve optimal results.

Benefits and Challenges
The integration of machine learning in compiler optimization offers profound benefits:

1. Enhanced Performance: Machine learning-driven compilers consistently achieve higher code performance by selecting optimizations tailored to specific code and hardware.

2. Reduced Development Effort: Developers no longer need to manually fine-tune code for performance, as

machine learning models automatically identify and apply optimizations.

3. Adaptability: Machine learning enables compilers to adapt to evolving codebases and target platforms, ensuring long-term performance improvements.

However, challenges remain:

1. Data Quality: Machine learning models require large, high-quality training datasets, which can be challenging to curate and maintain.

2. Model Interpretability: Understanding why a machine learning model makes specific optimization decisions is essential for debugging and code review.

3. Training Overhead: Building and training machine learning models can introduce overhead in the compilation process, potentially impacting development workflows.

Conclusion: The Code Efficiency Revolution
The integration of machine learning into compiler optimization represents a seismic shift in code efficiency. As machine learning models continue to evolve and compilers become more intelligent, software development will witness unparalleled performance gains, reduced developer burden, and optimized code for a multitude of platforms. The code efficiency revolution is here, and it promises to reshape the landscape of software development for years to come.

VI . Predictions and Future Directions in Compiler Design
Paving the Way for Tomorrow's Software
Compiler design, like the software it compiles, is not static. It evolves in response to technological

advancements, shifting paradigms, and the ever-growing demands of the software industry. In this section, we embark on a journey into the future, exploring predictions and emerging directions that will shape the landscape of compiler design.

1. Domain-Specific Languages (DSLs): Tailoring Compilers for Specialized Domains

As software becomes increasingly specialized, so too will the languages used to create it. Domain-specific languages (DSLs) are designed for specific application domains, such as machine learning, finance, or game development. In the future, compilers will adapt to accommodate the unique requirements of these DSLs. Expect to see more compiler generators and tools that enable the creation of DSLs, making it easier to build high-performance, domain-specific software.

2. Quantum Computing: Compilers for the Quantum Frontier

Quantum computing is on the horizon, promising unprecedented computational power. But it requires a new breed of compilers to harness this potential. Quantum compilers will need to optimize code for quantum algorithms, taking into account quantum gate operations and qubit entanglement. Expect quantum compiler research to flourish as quantum hardware becomes more accessible, paving the way for breakthroughs in cryptography, optimization, and materials science.

3. Security-First Compilers: Bolstering Software Resilience

As cyber threats grow in sophistication, so too must our defenses. Future compilers will integrate security measures at the code level. They will automatically detect and mitigate common vulnerabilities like buffer overflows, data leaks, and injection attacks. Expect security-first compilers to become essential in safeguarding software against an ever-expanding array of threats.

4. Explainable AI in Compilation: Understanding Compiler Decisions

Machine learning-driven compilers, while powerful, often operate as black boxes. In the future, explainable AI techniques will make compiler decisions more transparent. Developers will be able to understand why a compiler chose a particular optimization or transformation. This transparency is crucial for debugging and code review, and it will foster trust in AI-driven compilers.

5. Sustainable Computing: Compilers for Energy Efficiency

Energy efficiency is becoming a paramount concern in computing. Compilers will play a pivotal role in optimizing code for reduced energy consumption. Expect to see compilers that not only prioritize performance but also consider the environmental impact of software. Compiler-driven energy efficiency will be crucial for data centers, mobile devices, and IoT applications.

6. Polyglot Compilers: Bridging Language Barriers

Polyglot compilers, capable of understanding and optimizing code written in multiple programming languages, will become more prevalent. These compilers will enable seamless integration of diverse language ecosystems, facilitating interoperability and reducing the friction of using multiple languages within a single project.

7. Edge Computing: Compilers for Distributed Systems

The proliferation of edge computing, where processing occurs closer to data sources, will demand specialized compilers. These compilers will optimize code for edge devices with limited resources, ensuring efficient execution in distributed environments. Edge-focused compiler research will become critical for applications ranging from autonomous vehicles to IoT networks.

8. Continuous Compilation: Real-Time Adaptation
Continuous integration and continuous delivery (CI/CD) are the norm in modern software development. In the future, compilers will operate in a continuous compilation mode, adapting code as it evolves in real-time. This seamless integration with CI/CD pipelines will ensure that code remains optimized and efficient throughout its lifecycle.

Conclusion: Compiler Design at the Cutting Edge
Compiler design is a field of perpetual innovation, where the convergence of technology, theory, and industry needs reshapes the way we write and optimize software. As we peer into the future, these predictions and emerging directions in compiler design hint at a vibrant landscape of possibilities. Compiler engineers, researchers, and software developers are at the forefront of this journey, pioneering solutions that will shape the software of tomorrow and redefine the boundaries of what is achievable in computing.